Ask This Book a Question

An Interactive Journey to Find Wisdom
for Life's Big and Little Decisions

Written and illustrated by

Vicki Tan

A TarcherPerigee Book

an imprint of Penguin Random House LLC
1745 Broadway, New York, NY 10019
penguinrandomhouse.com

Copyright © 2025 by Vicki Tan
Penguin Random House values and supports copyright. Copyright fuels creativity,
encourages diverse voices, promotes free speech, and creates a vibrant culture.
Thank you for buying an authorized edition of this book and for complying
with copyright laws by not reproducing, scanning, or distributing any part of
it in any form without permission. You are supporting writers and allowing
Penguin Random House to continue to publish books for every reader.
Please note that no part of this book may be used or reproduced in any manner
for the purpose of training artificial intelligence technologies or systems.

TarcherPerigee with tp colophon is a registered trademark of
Penguin Random House LLC

Bias icon illustrations by Karen Yoojin Hong

Book and cover design by Vicki Tan

Library of Congress Cataloging-in-Publication Data
has been applied for.

Trade paperback ISBN: 9780593716960
Ebook ISBN: 9780593716977

Printed in the United States of America
1st Printing

The authorized representative in the EU for product safety and compliance is
Penguin Random House Ireland, Morrison Chambers, 32 Nassau Street,
Dublin D02 YH68, Ireland, https://eu-contact.penguin.ie.

For my family

In loving memory,
Jack 傳捷 Tan

Contents

Preface • xiii

Introduction • xv

How to Use This Book • xxiii

Questions • 1

Topic • 4

Timing • 18

Blockers • 26

A Big List of Questions • 34

Stories • 41

Charlie the Dog • 43

Buoyancy • 51

Mapo Tofu • 57

Yancey's Mustache • 63

Hanger Math • 67

Trim Grass • 73

Hsu Ken's Dad • 79

Trees • 85

Memory-Foam Pillow • 91

Slow Shopping • 97

Airport Optimism • 101

Good at Quitting • 107

Newness • 113

Full Circle • 119

The Rickshaw • 125

Doomscrolling • 133

Invariables • 139

Futureless • 145

Pentel 0.5mm Lead • 151

Biases • 157

Affective Forecasting • 158

Ambiguity Effect • 161

Anchoring Effect • 164

Appeal to Novelty • 167

Appeal to Probability • 170

Attentional Bias • 173

Availability Bias • 176

Bizarreness Effect • 179

Cathedral Effect • 182

Change Blindness • 185

Clustering Illusion • 188

Confirmation Bias • 191

Denomination Effect • 194

Dunning-Kruger Effect • 197

Effort Justification • 200

Endowment Effect • 203

Focusing Illusion • 206

Functional Fixedness • 209

Fundamental Attribution Error • 212

Halo Effect • 215

Hindsight Bias • 218

Hyperbolic Discounting • 221

Illusion of Control • 224

Illusory Truth Effect • 227

In-Group Bias • 230

Isolated Choice Effect • 233

Loss Aversion • 236

Mental Accounting • 239

Normalcy Bias • 242

Optimism Bias • 245

Peak-End Rule • 248

Post-Purchase Rationalization • 251

Recency Effect • 254

Restraint Bias • 257

Self-Licensing Effect • 260

Status Quo Bias • 263

Sunk Cost Fallacy • 266

Survivorship Bias • 269

Conclusion • 273

Acknowledgments • 275

Glossary of Biases • 277

There are years that ask questions
and years that answer.

—Zora Neale Hurston,
Their Eyes Were Watching God

Preface

Imagine wandering into a secondhand store in your favorite city, nestled on a quaint street across from a bakery known for its perfectly crumbly currant scones. As you navigate the shop's labyrinthine atrium, squeezing past crowded shelves in narrow aisles, your hand traces ornate frames, vintage typewriters, and old clocks frozen in time.

Tucked away in the back, an item piques your curiosity: a Magic 8 Ball. From a bygone era when people sought answers from the mystical, the one you hold in your hands is foggy with age, yet it possesses the same allure as those you remember. Instinctively, you do what countless others have done before you. You give it a shake and ask it your questions—everything from the profound to the ordinary.

But when you turn over this Magic 8 Ball for the answer, it offers you something different from the familiar responses you've come to expect—the traditional "yes," "outlook not so good," or "ask again later." Instead, its prompts encourage you along a journey of self-discovery, off your usual paths and through exciting, unmarked territory to help you find what you've been looking for.

This book is designed to be a little like that unusual Magic 8 Ball. Within these pages, you'll find a space to bring your questions and uncertainties, and through exploring them, you'll uncover far more than simple answers. Grounded in the science of cognitive biases and behavioral change, this book aims to help you find a new kind of wisdom—a deeper understanding of yourself that empowers you to approach life's most important decisions with confidence and clarity. It will help you become your own Magic 8 Ball.

Introduction

Each day, every one of us makes countless decisions. There are the daily, mundane choices you make based on your mood and circumstance: what to have for lunch, who to hang out with, what to do over the weekend. And then there are the bigger, more profound questions that you might mull over for years: how to be happy, how to overcome a fear, how to love.

The sum of different choices can bring you to life-changing decisions that serve as crossroads: whether to quit a job, whether to make a big move, whether to remain in a relationship. Every decision you make contributes to the larger narrative of who you are and who you're becoming.

The list of questions is infinite. There are decisions to make about work: how to balance the practical necessities of earning a living with the desire to find work that aligns with your values and passions. Questions about cultivating relationships: with family, friends, and romantic partners. Choices to make in your daily life: about your home, your health, your community. Not-yet-questions that are still unformed thoughts about your inner self: reflecting on your emotions, your values. Curiosity about the forces outside you that influence all this: chance and purpose and luck.

As we move through life, we naturally develop our own unique approaches for decision-making. These strategies fall along a vast spectrum. Some of us lean toward the objective, arming ourselves with the structure of lists and frameworks, breaking down each choice into its constituent parts. Others favor a more intuitive approach, talking with family and friends, applying wisdom learned from adages, and going by feel. And yet, our affinity toward one way or the other isn't static; we may oscillate between these approaches, shifting and adapting to the specific challenges we face, informed by the successes and failures of our past.

Paradoxically, we tend to apply more rigorous analysis to smaller, less consequential decisions, while relying on a loose calculus of gut feeling and advice for the most significant choices in our lives. We may agonize over which brand of electric toothbrush to buy, while making life-altering decisions about careers or relationships based on a hunch or a friend's opinion. We then may ruminate, second-guess ourselves, and worry over whether we've made the absolute best choice.

The truth is, most of us don't have a clear understanding of how to make decisions that genuinely align with our true wants and desires. Without a deeper grasp of what we're consciously choosing or passively surrendering to, we may find ourselves wondering, "How did I get here?" This realization is what inspired me to write this book.

My fascination with decision-making began during my university years when I discovered behavioral science. Unlike the objective lens of life science that I had originally planned to study, this branch of psychology felt more like a window into the subjective mysteries of the world.

After graduating, I started my career in research, working in academic hospitals at the University of California San Diego, my alma mater, as well as the University of California San Francisco and Stanford University. While spending time with patients was deeply fulfilling, I struggled with the lack of creativity inherent in my role. Conducting research demanded someone obsessed with consistency and rigorous detail, but my mind yearned for the stratosphere above, in the unconstrained space where imagination thrived. I wanted to be the one dreaming up novel ideas and uncovering better ways of doing things.

During this period of uncertainty, I sent out hundreds of applications like little directionless paper airplanes, each a hopeful message to the universe for jobs I wasn't quite qualified for. As if in response, a serendipitous opportunity at a large tech company presented itself—a three-month contract on an organizational psychology research team focused on finding creative, evidence-based methods to reduce bias in hiring. Despite the risk of leaving my full-time job during the recession of the early 2000s, the glimmer of opportunity was too enticing for me to pass up, a perfect alignment of the stars for my meandering career.

Tech proved to be the ideal industry for a dreamer like me, with years of pent-up ambition ready to burst forth. Working at this company offered sprawling, colorful campuses designed for play, seemingly endless extracurriculars to stimulate peripheral talents, and, most notably, its "20% Time" program. (This initiative encouraged employees to dedicate one day a week to a personal project of their choosing, with the only requirement being its potential benefit to the company.) My ideal scenario: designated curiosity-building time.

The gamble paid off. When I became a full-time employee, for the first time in my life I had the support of an incredibly smart manager who understood the value of uncovering and deepening our strengths. With her support, surrounded by a company full of talented designers to learn from, this is how I became a self-taught designer.

They say if you give a mouse a cookie, she's going to ask for a glass of milk. In that moment, I was very much that mouse who had gotten a taste of design—I wanted so much more.

As I transitioned from that big tech company to smaller startups for larger opportunities, I discovered that behavioral science and design were beautiful complements to each other—form and function coming together—and a natural extension of how my mind worked. In a sea of aspiring designers, this unique behavioral perspective became my defining differentiator, shaping my career path in unexpected ways and bringing me opportunities I couldn't have imagined back then (like writing this book!).

Product design offered the perfect canvas for blending the colors of human behavior with creative problem-solving. Each project became a creative challenge, inviting me to apply behavioral science principles in innovative ways.

One of the most rewarding examples of this was my work on a meditation app. Mindfulness, as many of us know, can be a daunting skill to master. It's easy to feel discouraged when our minds inevitably wander or when we struggle to find the time to practice during our busy days. By integrating habit anchors and motivational triggers into the app's onboarding process, I created a gentler way to ease new meditators into their meditation journey.

At another company, I faced the challenge of helping people build trust in a concept that was, at the time, quite novel: ridesharing. How could we encourage people to get into a stranger's car with confidence and ease? The key was shifting the mental models that people had about sharing rides. By designing interfaces that felt familiar and intuitive, and by communicating information in a way that resonated with their existing beliefs, we were able to foster a sense of trust and belonging that transcended the screen.

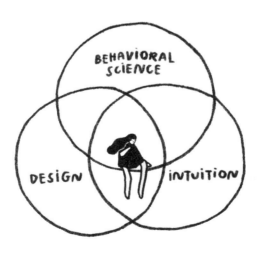

Since then, each of my professional experiences has been an experiment in blending behavioral science and design in different ways that deeply resonate with people. Now, I'm excited to channel this art and science of decision-making into this book. I'm reframing behavioral science through the lens of design thinking, making it more accessible and relatable to your everyday life. My goal is to offer you intuitive tools that will help you navigate life's choices with greater clarity and confidence.

We'll begin by exploring one of the most fascinating core concepts in this field, cognitive biases, and how they subtly yet powerfully shape our decisions every day.

If you've read anything about decision-making, you're likely familiar with the concept of cognitive biases—those mental shortcuts that can invisibly shape our behaviors and decisions. Often, these biases are stereotyped as mere psychological traps, leading us astray and clouding our judgment. However, the approach I offer in this book isn't simply about eliminating these biases—an impossible task, really—but about seeing them in a new light. Embracing this potential is an exercise not in letting the worst aspect of something be the crescendo, but rather in seeing what else might emerge.

Research on motivation shows that viewing these tendencies as essential parts of ourselves, with both bright and dark aspects, allows us to be less at odds with them and better equipped to navigate their influence. In this way, my exploration of these biases extends beyond their traditional scientific definitions.

While grounded in research, I've taken creative liberty, through storytelling and open-ended framing, to make these concepts more relatable.

At their core, biases are mental shortcuts that we've developed to help us make sense of the world. They're the survival instincts that help us spot patterns, navigate uncertainty, and handle complexity. These cognitive strategies help us learn from the past, adapt to the present, and prepare for the future. By simplifying the vast information we encounter daily, these mental models help us focus, prioritize, and make decisive choices. The key is understanding when to challenge our instincts and when to trust our gut.

While cognitive biases can be useful, overreliance on them can lead to negative cycles, unfair judgments, and limited growth. Developing an awareness of this dichotomy will help you develop the intuition to make choices that align with your values, embracing both sides of yourself to see what new insights might emerge.

So, when you find yourself with a stubborn decision or in a challenging situation—ask this book a question. Ask the hopeful, challenging, and quiet queries you've held on to, and then learn how to move forward with them in a deeper way. By gaining insight into how your mind perceives and makes judgments about the world, you can start to connect with yourself to see what you're truly choosing.

Just like that unusual Magic 8 Ball you discovered in the quaint shop, this book will be your guide as you navigate life's uncertainties. With each question you ask and each page you turn, you'll develop the wisdom within yourself. This intuition will be your guide to help you approach your most important decisions with clarity and confidence.

How to Use This Book

What kinds of questions can you ask of this book? The best ones are those you might ask an advice column or even a fortune teller. I can't help with factual queries you'd ask Google, or predictive questions about the weather or winning lottery numbers—if only! What I want are your deep life questions that you discuss with your closest friends and that fill the pages of your journal.

QUESTION   STORY   BIAS

Each question in this book will lead you to a personal story, a fable crafted to share my favorite life lessons. These narratives serve as mnemonic devices, helping you understand behavioral science concepts in a relatable, human way. Throughout each story, you'll find cognitive biases highlighted, revealing how they can influence your choices and perceptions in subtle ways.

After each story, you can learn about each of these biases in more depth by flipping to their page in the last section of the book.

(Some questions will also lead directly to a bias.) Cognitive biases are like lenses that color our perception and decision-making. Just as a lens can bring things into focus or distort our vision, biases can have both positive and negative effects on our choices. In the "light" and "shadow" sections, which explore the positive and negative aspects of each bias, you'll discover how these mental shortcuts can look in different situations, and how they can either sharpen our judgment or lead us astray. I've also included targeted questions, journaling prompts, and real-life examples to teach you about the complex interplay of emotions, intuition, and reasoning that underlies your choices, empowering you to navigate life's challenges with greater clarity and intention.

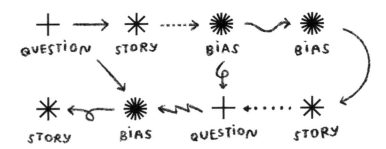

The navigation in this book is designed to be organic and intuitive, allowing you to explore the content in a way that feels natural and engaging. The questions in the first part of the book act as signposts, guiding you toward the stories and biases that resonate most with your current situation and state of mind. If you're the type of reader who prefers a more structured or linear approach, you can of course read the book from beginning to end. This path may feel more like wandering through a museum, each chapter a self-contained exhibit inviting you to explore a particular theme.

As you explore the book, allow yourself to be guided by your curiosity. This is your journey, and the path you take will be distinctly your own. Trust that the questions and stories that draw your attention are the ones that hold the most valuable lessons for you in this moment.

To get the most out of your reading experience:

- Keep a journal or digital notes to jot down your thoughts, reflections, and questions.

- Actively engage with the material by underlining passages that resonate with you, responding to prompts, and doodling your feelings.

- When new questions emerge, use the bias pages as a quick reference guide.

Once you've finished the book, keep it close at hand, on your coffee table as a visual totem to remind you of what you've learned. Revisit these pages as your life situations change, forging meaningful connections between the book's insights and your own experiences.

Ultimately, my hope is that this book will be a catalyst for personal growth and discovery. Embrace the detours, the aha moments, and the questions that arise along the way—they are all essential parts of your unique path.

+ QUESTIONS +

Your journey begins with a question—a puzzling thought, a persistent challenge, or a desire for clarity. Use these visual prompts as an intuitive navigation tool, to encourage a more organic approach to explore your question from new angles.

Think of your question as the starting point of an adventure—one that invites you to wander off the usual paths, discover hidden connections, and embrace obstacles. Follow the tangents that capture your interest, even if they lead you in unexpected directions. At this stage, your only goal is to expand your perspective, and find where to go next.

By approaching your question from different vantage points, you may uncover the underlying reasons why it has been so challenging for you. Let go of the expectation of quick answers. You might be surprised by what happens when you allow yourself to get a little lost.

Remember, this is a dynamic, interactive experience. Feel free to jump around, linger on prompts that resonate with you, and revisit them as your understanding evolves. Trust your intuition, and let your curiosity be your guide.

Think of a question . . .

It should be something that's been calling to you. Maybe it's been hard to grasp or you've been caught in indecision. If multiple questions come to mind, start with one and come back to the others later. (If you don't have a question yet, skip to number 4.)

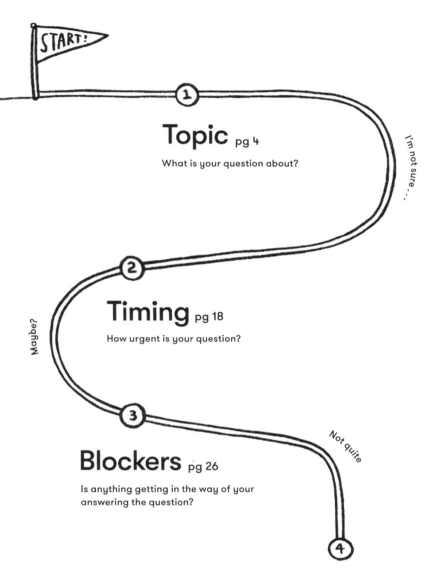

START!

①

Topic pg 4

What is your question about?

I'm not sure . . .

②

Timing pg 18

How urgent is your question?

Maybe?

③

Blockers pg 26

Is anything getting in the way of your answering the question?

Not quite

④

A big list of questions pg 34

If nothing is calling to you, take a look through questions others have asked.

1. Topic

What is your question about?

If you've picked up this book with a burning question on your mind, start by considering whether it falls under one of these broad yet essential categories: Everyday Life, Health, Relationships, Work, Quality Time, or Existential.

While not an exhaustive list, these high-level areas can serve as a starting point for your exploration. As you explore the following visuals, allow yourself to be drawn into the interconnectedness of these themes.

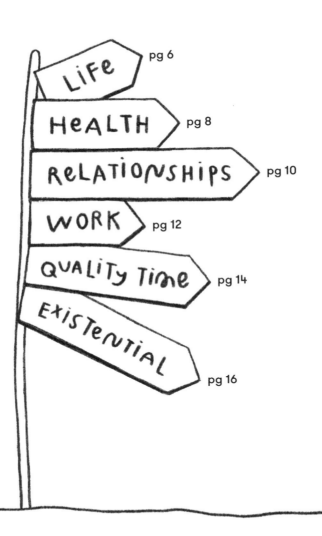

LiFe — pg 6

HeALTH — pg 8

ReLATiONSHiPS — pg 10

WORK — pg 12

QuALiTy TiMe — pg 14

EXisTeNTiAL — pg 16

Life

If your question is about your everyday life, consider the routines that shape your days. There's often comfort in the familiar cycle: waking up, going to work, spending time with others, sharing meals, and then returning home to sleep. Within this rhythm, take a moment to notice what has become habitual or perhaps escaped your attention. Decide which parts you want to keep doing intentionally each day.

Occasionally, a big transition will shake things all up. When this happens, it's an opportunity to adapt and reevaluate your daily patterns before settling back into a new rhythm of life.

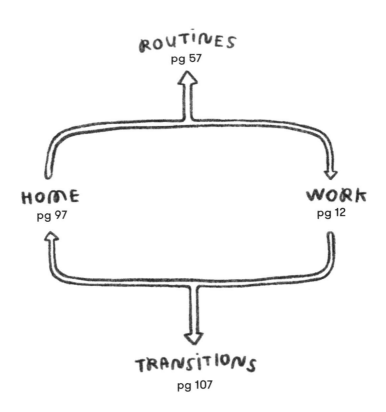

ROUTINES
pg 57

HOME
pg 97

WORK
pg 12

TRANSITIONS
pg 107

Health

If your question relates to your health, notice how health is a perpetual balance of your internal and external states. This means taking care of your mind and body through what you put in it each day, how you move and interact with your surroundings, and who you spend time with. Your physical health, including exercise and your gut's microbiome, can influence your emotions, which in turn can affect your mental health and how you feel when you wake up each day. The cumulative effects of your short-term choices will manifest in different ways over your lifetime.

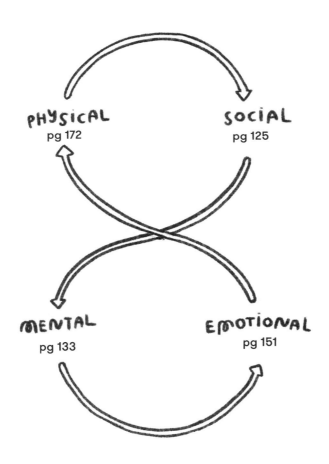

PHYSICAL
pg 172

SOCIAL
pg 125

MENTAL
pg 133

EMOTIONAL
pg 151

Relationships

If your question is about relationships, keep in mind that we are social creatures, and relationships are deeply ingrained in our nature. In our earliest moments, our sense of self and attachment is shaped by our parents or caretakers, helping us develop an understanding of love, trust, and intimacy. As we grow older, we learn to navigate the complexity of friendship and romantic love, each connection adding another layer in our growing understanding of others and ourselves. Whether you choose to have a family or surround yourself with chosen family, you build a community with these individuals through a lifetime of shared experiences and deepening commitments.

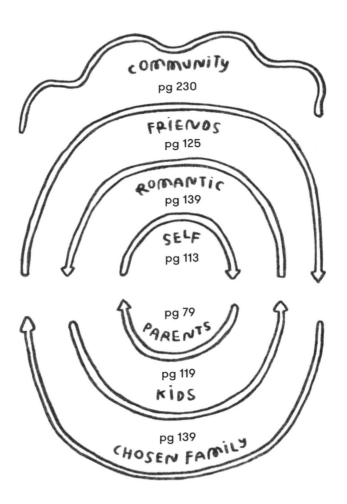

COMMUNITY
pg 230

FRIENDS
pg 125

ROMANTIC
pg 139

SELF
pg 113

pg 79
PARENTS

pg 119
KIDS

pg 139
CHOSEN FAMILY

Work

If your question is about work or money, notice how these areas can feel like a perpetual upward climb. We search for jobs early in our career, and these can set us on a path toward professional growth and can shape our identity. Our work is also how we earn a living, and we need to find balance in how we choose to spend and save our money. As our earning potential increases, it can be natural to upgrade our life and indulge in new luxuries, which in turn requires us to make more money. This hedonic treadmill can make it feel like we are trapped in unfulfilling jobs and careers, affecting our health and leading to burnout. When this happens, we may look for an emergency escape hatch, freeing us from the vertical grind and allowing us to reconsider how to begin again.

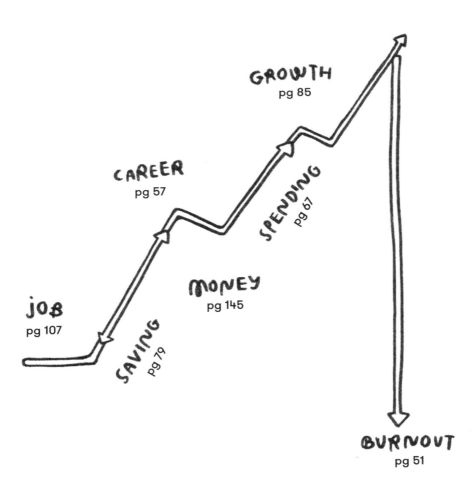

GROWTH
pg 85

CAREER
pg 57

SPENDING
pg 67

JOB
pg 107

SAVING
pg 79

MONEY
pg 145

BURNOUT
pg 51

Quality Time

If your question is about quality time, consider what you naturally gravitate toward, in between obligations. Pay attention to what gives you energy, what feels light and restful. While these activities don't necessarily have to be fun and relaxing, they should have a quality that fills your cup at the end of the day. For some, this means spending time with others, traveling to new places, or enjoying nature. For others, it can involve learning a new instrument or language, or engaging in projects like building a shed or writing poetry. Quality time can also be subtle—being still, sitting with your thoughts, and feeling synchronous with your surroundings.

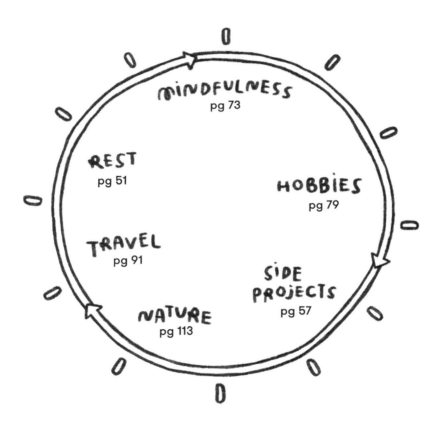

MINDFULNESS
pg 73

REST
pg 51

HOBBIES
pg 79

TRAVEL
pg 91

SIDE
PROJECTS
pg 57

NATURE
pg 113

Existential

If your question is more existential in nature, you may not have fully conceptualized it yet, making it harder to untangle where it begins and ends. It may revolve around your emotions, ranging from intense to subtle, and how they're deeply connected to your sense of self and self-perception. You might be grappling with understanding the purpose and overall meaning of life and considering the role of chance, fate, and personal agency in shaping your path. These questions are often interconnected and seemingly unanswerable in some way, leading you to revisit them at different stages throughout your life.

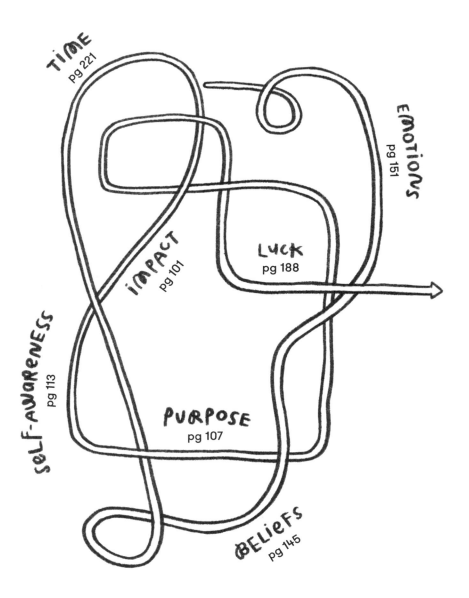

TIME
pg 221

EMOTIONS
pg 151

IMPACT
pg 101

LUCK
pg 188

SELF-AWARENESS
pg 113

PURPOSE
pg 107

BELIEFS
pg 145

2. Timing

How urgent is your question?

Consider the time sensitivity of your decision. For example, choosing a college major is less urgent than choosing whether to accept a time-sensitive job offer.

EVENTUAL · URGENT

Eventual questions may not have a deadline or urgency attached to them. These often relate to long-term goals, personal growth, or lifestyle changes. You might keep these in the back of your mind for years.

Urgent questions demand immediate answers due to time constraints or other pressing circumstances. These require quick decisions and often involve health, safety, or critical opportunities.

How often does this question arise?

Think about how frequently you face this type of decision. For example, choosing what to have for dinner is more frequent than deciding to buy a house.

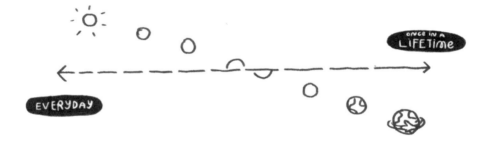

Everyday questions are those you consider daily, such as what to wear, how to manage your time, what to eat, and how to communicate with others. You have the opportunity to answer these questions repeatedly.

Once-in-a-lifetime questions arise infrequently and often involve significant life changes, rare opportunities, or major milestones. You may have only a few chances to answer these questions throughout your life.

Putting It Together

By combining the ideas of urgency (how quickly we need to decide) and frequency (how often we face similar choices), we can use a new lens for examining why certain decisions take more time than others, or why some seem to slip our mind.

Long-term reflective questions

- Big-picture questions about life goals and dreams, often without set deadlines.
- For these complex decisions, set time for reflection and break them into smaller steps toward long-term goals.

Now or never questions

- Major, one-time decisions that demand immediate attention and can have significant consequences.
- Stay levelheaded, avoid impulsive choices, and seek support from trusted advisers for these high-stakes decisions.

Routine decisions

- Habitual, regular choices about daily life made without much thought.
- Being intentional about these decisions can lead to meaningful improvements over time.

Pressing matters

- Urgent, daily micro-decisions requiring quick action.
- Prioritize the most critical issues and develop strategies for handling repeated interruptive tasks.

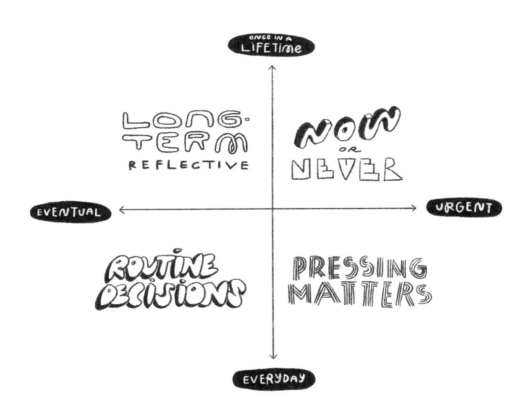

Potential Pitfalls

While understanding the characteristics and strategies that are best for each type of decision can help us navigate them more effectively, it's equally important to be aware of the potential pitfalls.

Rumination

- Prone to overthinking, indecision, or decision paralysis.
- Risk of getting stuck in abstract planning without taking concrete action steps.

All-consuming

- Can lead to feeling overwhelmed or constantly putting out fires.
- Risk of neglecting important long-term priorities in favor of urgent short-term demands.

Easily overlooked

- Easy to miss opportunities for improvement due to their habitual nature.
- Risk of getting stuck in suboptimal patterns or failing to adapt to changing circumstances.

Time suck

- High-pressure situations that can lead to impulsive or panic-driven choices.
- Risk of making suboptimal decisions due to time constraints and limited perspective.

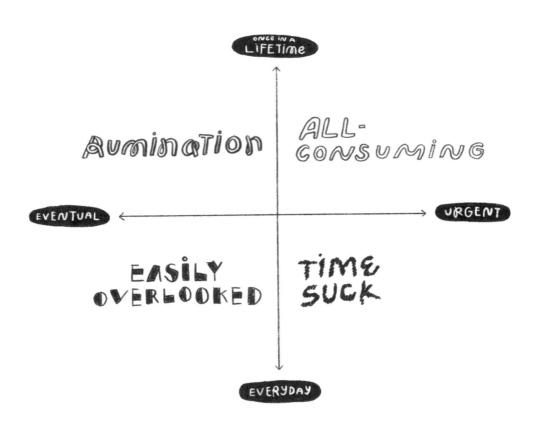

Example Questions

These questions illustrate how the timing, urgency, and long-term versus short-term nature of a decision can impact why we might be overthinking something or not giving enough attention to it at all. They also help us understand why certain ones seem to take up all our time and energy.

For instance, a **long-term reflective question** that may result in **rumination** could be *"How do I face my greatest fears?"* because there's no urgency in answering it, as long as you avoid the fear. On the other hand, **now-or-never questions** such as *"Should I accept this job offer?"* quickly become **all-consuming** because they take our attention away from everything else until we resolve them.

Similarly, **routine decisions** that don't have a matter of urgency like *"Am I wasting time?"* may be **easily overlooked** day after day because the thought occurs to us so frequently that we become used to dismissing or deprioritizing answering it. Conversely, **pressing matters** can create daily mini fire drills, making us wonder *"Why am I so busy?"* because they can become a **time suck** within themselves.

By considering the characteristics of the question along these dimensions—its urgency, long-term importance, and complexity—we can match and adjust our approach to the demands of the question.

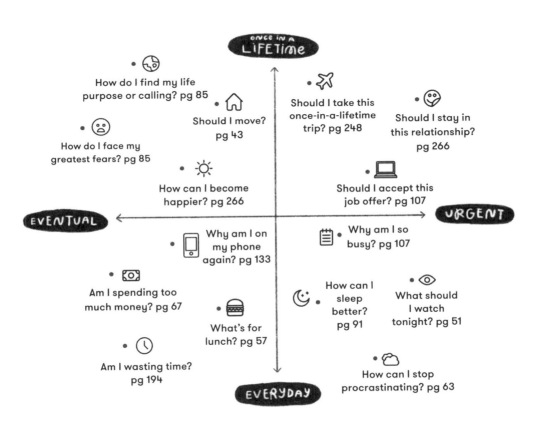

ONCE IN A LIFETIME

How do I find my life purpose or calling? pg 85

Should I move? pg 43

How do I face my greatest fears? pg 85

How can I become happier? pg 266

Should I take this once-in-a-lifetime trip? pg 248

Should I stay in this relationship? pg 266

Should I accept this job offer? pg 107

EVENTUAL

URGENT

Why am I on my phone again? pg 133

Why am I so busy? pg 107

Am I spending too much money? pg 67

How can I sleep better? pg 91

What should I watch tonight? pg 51

What's for lunch? pg 57

Am I wasting time? pg 194

How can I stop procrastinating? pg 63

EVERYDAY

3. Blockers

Is anything getting in the way of your answering the question?

If you're struggling to answer your question, it might simply mean that you need to give attention to the part that is stuck. As you explore these pages, pay attention to when the answers come easily and when something feels off or challenging to answer. When we encounter blocks, our frustration can cause us to push them away or assume things are stuck that way. Instead, use these prompts to embrace your obstacles and look to them as clues for which direction to go from here.

Intuition

Can you trust your gut? Can you follow your internal compass?

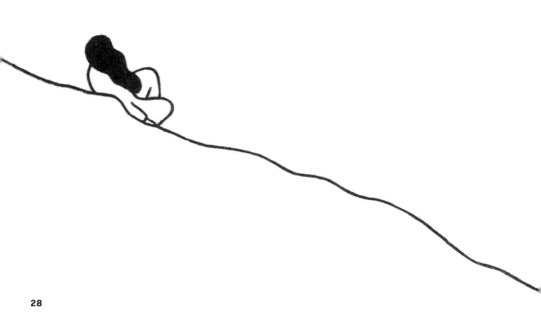

Resources

Do you have the time and money to address your question?

Skills

Do you have the skills and knowledge to address your question?

Support

Are you able to talk to your friends, family, and community? Are they supportive of your asking the question?

Emotions

Do you feel emotionally prepared to dig deeper into this? Do you have the mental capacity to work through this situation?

Impact

Will the question you're asking have far-reaching consequences beyond yourself? Will it affect people around you, the environment, or the future?

4. A Big List of Questions

Not sure where to start? Haven't found a question that resonates with you? That's okay. This list of questions, gathered from friends and acquaintances during my research, might uncover topics you haven't yet realized are important to you. Each question points to a specific page, and while it may not perfectly match your situation, it can serve as a useful starting point for this exploration.

Life

- What do I want right now? **pg 73**
- Why am I so busy? **pg 107**
- How can I be more present? **pg 113**
- How can I stop procrastinating? **pg 63**
- What's for lunch? **pg 57 and 233**
- What should I do tonight? **pg 194 and 263**
- Should I adopt a pet? **pg 43**
- How can I best prepare for a big life transition? **pg 158**
- How do I share chores and labor with my household? **pg 265**
- What should I wear today? **pg 67**
- How can I put what I read and learn into practice in my daily life? **pg 51**

- Where is home? **pg 139**
- Should I move? **pg 43**
- Where should I live? **pg 218**
- How can I have more structure but not have to follow so many rules for myself? **pg 79**
- What can I do on a daily basis to meaningfully impact the world (climate, community, etc.)? **pg 242**

Health

- How can I be healthier? **pg 221 and 257**
- Am I getting enough rest? **pg 113**
- Why am I so tired? **pg 133**
- Do I drink too much? **pg 185**
- How can I stop overthinking or ruminating? **pg 73, 206, and 224**
- How do I deal with emotions like anger, fear, anxiety, and sadness? **pg 73, 133, and 151**
- How can I resist unhealthy eating and drinking to support the life I want? **pg 257 and 260**
- How can I be less impulsive? **pg 97, 167, and 257**
- How can I break out of a cycle of burnout? **pg 266**
- How can I regain my energy? **pg 113**
- Why do I feel stressed? **pg 133**
- How can I become happier? **pg 266**
- How do I train my body and mind for a healthy long life? **pg 51**
- What can I do today that I will thank myself for in a year? **pg 221**

Relationships

- Do I have a healthy relationship with myself and others? **pg 212 and 215**
- How can I stay more connected to the people around me? **pg 254**
- What does it mean to love? **pg 139**
- How do I heal from heartbreak? **pg 248**
- How can I be more considerate of others? **pg 101**
- How can I be less frustrated with others? **pg 212**
- Should I break up with my partner? **pg 200 and 266**
- How can I make new friends? **pg 230**
- How can I form deeper relationships? **pg 125**
- Who is my chosen family? **pg 139**
- How will I meet my life partner? **pg 161**
- Should I get married? **pg 139**

Family

- How can I create an environment that allows my children to thrive? **pg 79**
- Should I become a parent? **pg 119**
- How do I balance my family's needs with my personal needs? **pg 245**
- How can I care for my aging parents? **pg 242**
- How can I be a better partner, friend, and/or parent? **pg 254**

Money

- How do I budget for a big purchase while still meeting my other financial goals? **pg 239**
- How can I be more intentional in what I buy? **pg 67 and 251**
- How can I become financially secure? **pg 79**
- How do I set financial goals and stick to them? **pg 57**
- How do I invest wisely? **pg 197**
- How can I spend less and live within my means? **pg 145**
- How do I save more money? **pg 194 and 251**
- Should I make this big purchase? **pg 97**
- Am I spending too much money? **pg 67**
- Am I making enough money? **pg 239**
- Should I buy or rent my home? **pg 227**

Work

- Should I quit my job? **pg 266**
- Is there a more fulfilling job out there for me? **pg 107**
- Should I change my career path? **pg 57 and 245**
- Am I willing to take a pay cut to live a slower, more stress-free life? **pg 57**
- How do I balance my career goals with my family life? **pg 245**
- How can I be more productive and achieve my goals? **pg 182**
- Am I taking enough time off? **pg 57**
- How do I decide what to say no to? **pg 107**
- How do I become adaptable in my work? **pg 79 and 209**

- How can I feel my creative energy again? **pg 182**
- Should I go back to school? **pg 161 and 176**
- How can I be more intentional with what I learn? **pg 79 and 245**
- How do I find my path in life? **pg 85**
- How can I best use my skills and talents? **pg 209**
- How can I set aspirational but useful career goals? **pg 269**

Quality time

- How can I make more time for family and friends? **pg 194**
- How should I spend my free time? **pg 194**
- How do I make time for all my interests and passions? **pg 107**
- How can I become inspired? **pg 73 and 113**
- How can I remove myself from situations that disempower me and take away my energy? **pg 107**
- Where has all my time gone? **pg 51**
- How can I have a healthy relationship with social media? **pg 73 and 133**
- Why am I on social media again? **pg 179**
- How can I make travel more personally meaningful? **pg 73**
- How can I make time for personal projects? **pg 194**
- How do I decide which interest or passion to focus on first? **pg 176**
- How should I spend my holiday, vacation, or time off? **pg 248**

Existential

- How can I be more courageous? **pg 91**

- How can I improve my self-esteem and confidence? **pg 63 and 85**
- How can I find more meaning and fulfillment in my life? **pg 170**
- How do I find my life's purpose or calling? **pg 85**
- Does everything work out in the end? **pg 158 and 218**
- How can I be more prepared for the future? **pg 101**
- How can I balance what I need with what I want? **pg 51 and 221**
- How can I create environments where I thrive? **pg 91 and 97**
- Why do I feel sad? **pg 151**
- What do I do when I'm feeling stuck? **pg 73**
- How do I deal with my anxiety? **pg 158**
- How do I find joy? **pg 113**
- What's the most important thing right now? **pg 176**
- How can I trust in myself? **pg 91**
- How can I be more open-minded? **pg 164 and 191**
- How do I face my biggest fears? **pg 85**
- Am I wasting time? **pg 194**
- How can I be more patient? **pg 79 and 221**
- How do I become lucky? **pg 161**
- Why do coincidences feel magical? **pg 179**
- How can I be more motivated? **pg 63**
- How can I let things go? **pg 173**
- How can I be more minimal? **pg 203**
- How do I deal with loss? **pg 236**
- How can I find meaning in failure? **pg 269**

✳ STORIES ✳

Stories are how we make meaning; they can bring cohesion to our narratives and become lenses through which we understand our lives. The stories in this book illuminate the messy, human, and unexpected ways that our biases manifest in real situations, offering profound lessons to guide you in navigating your own experiences.

These narratives, drawn from my personal journey and the lives of friends and mentors, intertwine playful storytelling with insights from cognitive biases. While your circumstances may differ from mine, these stories are designed to spark your curiosity about how understanding biases can deepen your connection to the choices you make.

As you immerse yourself in these stories, pay attention to how they resonate with your own life, and consider how your unique blend of history, personality, quirks, comforts, routines, inclinations, and luck has shaped your personal narrative. Use them as a catalyst for self-reflection and discovery, recognizing that biases are not abstract concepts but deeply ingrained influences that color our perceptions and guide our actions.

Charlie the Dog

+ QUESTIONS

- Should I adopt a pet?
- Should I move?

At the start of the pandemic, like many other socially isolated people with an abundance of free time, I decided to adopt a dog. I told the rescue that I was looking for a medium-sized, active companion—one who would enjoy jogs and weekend hikes but would also be content napping while I worked during the day. Yet somehow, I ended up bringing home a lumbering 150-pound Great Pyrenees named Charlie. With his thick and fluffy white coat, enormous size, and gentle demeanor, Charlie looks more like a friendly polar bear than your average dog.

The owner of the rescue was an eccentric retired corporate lawyer who drove up with Charlie in her vintage Mercedes-Benz, his huge head poking out the back window. As we talked, she claimed to sense a connection between me and the bear, and nudged me to take him home. I was skeptical—Charlie was massive! My mind immediately raced with logistical questions: How would I manage all that fur? How much food does he eat? What if I needed to carry him? Owning a dog that weighed more than me seemed daunting, but the owner's enthusiasm was contagious. She offered that I could start by fostering him, and if I didn't feel like I could manage, I could always give him back.

Over the next few months, I figured out how to be a Big

Dog Mom™. I invested in a high-powered vacuum for his fur. I learned that, despite his size, he only eats about four cups of kibble a day (an average amount for dogs). And over time, what became most noticeable wasn't his outward appearance, but his remarkably calm disposition.

Though reportedly only two years old at the time, Charlie carried himself with the peaceful air of a wise old soul. He is always content to wait patiently until his next walk, snoozing on the couch without complaints. On our strolls, Charlie frequently pauses to investigate the usual high-traffic poles and mark important bushes. But unlike other dogs, he moves at an unhurried pace, often stopping for a full minute to take deep inhales of flowers, completely unperturbed by yapping passersby and loud city noises.

These meandering walks became an unexpected source of joy. Despite living in my hilly neighborhood for a decade, I had never explored it so extensively. With my large companion, I discovered hidden gems I'd somehow overlooked all these years. We uncovered concrete slides tucked away in parks, stumbled upon a thriving community garden, and found secret staircases that offered shortcuts to hilltop views. What began as a necessity quickly evolved into a grounding routine. I found myself looking forward to these peaceful outings, grateful for the fresh air and the gentle nudge to step outside morning, noon, and night. Charlie was here to stay.

During the lockdown period, the delivery guy was a frequent streetside visitor. After dropping off packages, he would always yell a farewell "Falkor!,"[1] his voice fading into the distance as he drove off, chuckling to himself, feeling clever for making the connection between Charlie and the flying luck dragon from *The NeverEnding Story.*

Reactions like these are typical. I can't walk for more than fifteen minutes without someone asking me a question about Charlie. "What kind of dog is that?" "How old is he?" "Does he shed a lot?" And there's always the one-liners: "Who's walking who?" *wink, wink* And my favorite, "You got a saddle for your horse?" Sometimes people will simply stop in their tracks to tell me that he is the biggest dog they've ever seen. Other times, their reactions are subtle—an unabashed smile, a tap on a companion's shoulder, a covert photo taken as evidence of a day brightened after catching sight of Charlie's friendly gait coming toward them.

Charlie has an uncanny ability to jump-start conversations with any stranger, stopping even the most hurried New Yorker in their tracks. Grown men have stooped to kiss his head. Cranky bodega owners have whispered sweet nothings in his ear. Adults and children alike fawn over him. It's what I imagine walking around with a child star or D-list celebrity must be like.

As you might imagine, this can be sweet, amusing, embarrassing, and annoying—all at once, depending how busy, in a rush, or tired I am.

---

1 Falkor is a luck dragon from the movie *The NeverEnding Story.* He is a wise, optimistic, dignified, friendly, sophisticated creature from Fantasia who gives advice when people have lost hope in what they set out to do.

On its own, adopting a dog is a big responsibility that comes with lessons in parenting and loving another creature. On top of that, the benefits for health and longevity are worthwhile, for sure. But owning an extra-large dog like Charlie has taught me something more meaningful: how to slow down, how to lean into unexpected interactions, and how to cultivate empathy toward others.

You see, with an average dog, you might run into an occasional dog lover who wants to give a passing scratch. But walking around with a polar bear lookalike invites another level of social interaction: those exclamations of delight, amazement, surprise, and even awe. This constant exchange with strangers requires a type of patience and humility that I have learned to channel from the big guy himself.

Because I'm with Charlie every day, he looks like a normal dog to me. But then I remember not everyone else sees the world how I see it. So, each time someone asks me a Charlie question, it gently pulls me right out of my first-person mental bubble. Each interaction becomes an opportunity to see the world through someone else's eyes, even if just for a moment.

Instead of becoming irritated, I've learned to appreciate the joy Charlie brings to others, understanding that what's routine for me can be extraordinary for them (EGOCENTRIC BIAS). Through these daily encounters, he's helped me practice shifting my mindset—from self-focused to other-focused, from impatience to understanding, from rushing through life to appreciating small, unexpected connections. I've learned to accept interruptions as opportunities to let go of my own agenda, if only briefly, to share in someone else's excitement and curiosity (ATTENTIONAL BIAS).

These experiences with Charlie have made me reflect on how we often approach change in our lives.

When we're in a rut, we tend to seek big, declarative moves. We change our cities, our jobs, and our relationships because it feels good to start a new chapter. There's a certain allure to making a change on paper and thinking, "When I move *here*, then I'll be able to do this," or "Once I'm in *this* role, I'll be satisfied." I'm all too familiar with these if only statements, as I've had repeated firsthand experiences seeking out sweeping life changes, international moves, and more in hope of a resulting vibe shift.[2]

The thing is . . . while big moves can lead to lasting changes, they can often distract us from the subtler internal work that needs to be done. As humans, we have a funny habit of explaining our behaviors by looking at our external circumstances, rather than examining our own character (FUNDAMENTAL ATTRIBUTION ERROR). By prioritizing dramatic lifestyle shifts with immediate impacts, we can inadvertently lose sight of what we need to work on. These are often smaller adjustments, very specific to us, that have a longer timeline for change. My daily walks with Charlie exemplify Rick Rubin's concept of "sustainable rituals that create openness and awareness for you."

---

2 The fresh start effect is a psychological phenomenon where people are more likely to pursue goals or make positive changes at significant time markers (e.g., New Year's Day, birthdays, or starting a new job). These moments are perceived as new beginnings, creating mental separation from past failures and boosting motivation for self-improvement.

So, the next time you're itching to make a radical life overhaul, pause and investigate. Ask yourself: Is this change addressing the root of your dissatisfaction, or is it just a surface-level fix? Consider incorporating daily practices that open you up to new perspectives: take a walk in a different neighborhood without headphones, volunteer with a group outside your usual social circles, or attend a community event you wouldn't normally go to. Start with something manageable—maybe not adopting a huge dog like Charlie, but perhaps trying a new hobby that challenges you.

Through these intentional, everyday changes, you may find your perspective shifting in subtle ways, like you might welcome an interruption as an opportunity to connect with a stranger and see the world through their eyes. Sometimes, the biggest transformations come not from grand gestures or external overhauls but from deepening our engagement with the world around us, one giant, fluffy pet at a time.

✳ BIASES TO EXPLORE

Egocentric bias:
We sometimes rely too heavily on our own perspective and have a higher opinion of ourselves than we'd have about someone else who was exactly like us.

Attentional bias, pg 173:
If we think about something, we'll notice it more in our day-to-day.

Fundamental attribution error, pg 212:
We tend to attribute other people's behavior to their personality rather than to external circumstances.

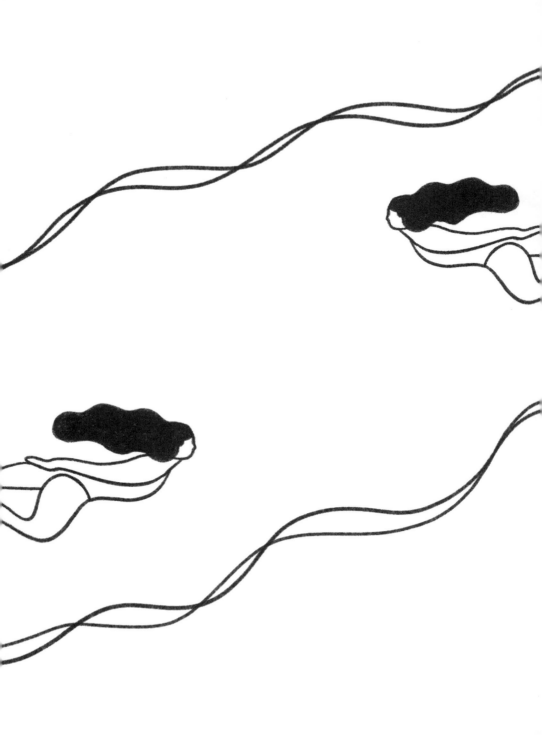

Buoyancy

+ QUESTIONS

- How can I put what I read and learn into practice in my daily life?
- How do I train my body and mind for a healthy long life?
- Where has all my time gone?
- How can I balance what I need with what I want?

Scuba diving has always felt like the closest I will ever get to being in outer space. As I descend deeper below the surface, my visual awareness heightens and sounds become muted as the world transforms into a shimmering array of aquamarine. I start to notice the shift in environment as everything moves more gently, with an otherworldly hypnotism, as if gravity has loosened its grip. In this state of near weightlessness, suspended underwater, I find myself enveloped by new topographies and the mesmerizing swirl of strange and magnificent creatures— the intricate patterning on a nudibranch, the iridescent flutter of a cuttlefish. Diving has become one of my favorite hobbies, an escape into a realm where the rules of the world above no longer apply.

To become a certified diver, one of the many things you must master is your *buoyancy*. When you maintain neutral buoyancy, you can swim underwater at a constant depth, similar to how an airplane flies at a constant altitude. Many factors impact your buoyancy that you can adjust and accommodate for on land: your wet suit's thickness, the weight of your gear, and your body mass composition. But once you're in the ocean, buoyancy is controlled almost exclusively by you—by your breath.

As you breathe in, you fill your lungs with air. The oxygen in your lungs causes you to slowly float up toward the surface. Each time you breathe out, you expel oxygen, which in turn causes you to float down toward the seafloor. By taking slow and continuous breaths, you can offset these up-and-down oscillations, which allows you to maintain a steady path as you move around underwater.

Learning to dive can be challenging for many reasons—in particular, how foreign the sensation feels. When you find yourself meters below the surface for the first time, you may start to feel nervous and overthink how unnatural it is to be that far down.

Wearing all that gear with dials and knobs can cause you to catastrophize about everything that could go awry (ATTENTIONAL BIAS). Then your heart starts to pound faster and your breath quickens. And to make matters worse, the additional air you're rapidly taking in makes you more buoyant, and your anxiety is further magnified as you unintentionally float upward. All of a sudden, your own body is out of your control. And when diving, you know that you have to be careful to ascend slowly because of the compressed nitrogen in the air that's in your brain and body.

Scuba diving heightens your awareness of your internal state by physically manifesting it through your body's positioning in the water. When you're nervous or anxious, you might breathe faster and inadvertently take in more air, causing you to float upward. Can you imagine if this happened on land? If you got nervous and started floating up in the air? It would be so much more embarrassing than sweaty palms! This attunement to feeling what's going on inside your body is called *interoception*. As you're sitting here reading this, take a moment to observe your interoceptive senses. Can you sense if you're tense or relaxed in various parts of your body? Try to notice if your breath is shallow or deep, or if you're breathing into your lungs or your belly. Pay attention to the rate at which your heart is beating.

As I've gotten more experience underwater, the concept of buoyancy has started to feel more like second nature and has given me access to different, more advanced dives and a whole new level of ocean access. One of my most vivid memories was at a volcanic island off the coast of Malaysia called Sipadan. A volcanic island is exactly what it sounds like—a volcano that sits underwater on the seafloor, with its top poking up just enough to reveal a land mass. Sipadan is especially unusual because it's anchored at the *deep* sea level, starting at two thousand meters down (that's over a mile!).

This makes the island extremely long and thin, which creates these currents of water that carry you along the face of the rock at top speeds. It was here that I found myself engulfed in a school of barracuda. They surrounded me, forming a shimmering, hurricane-shaped cone as they moved in unison. Despite knowing their predatory behavior, I didn't feel scared. The barracudas' lateralis systems—sensory organs that allow fish to detect movement and pressure changes in the water—enabled them to navigate effortlessly around me in proximity but never touching.

The counterpart to interoception, or your ability to sense your inner state, is *exteroception*: how you're taking in information from your external world and stimuli. When you're underwater, you might be breathing quickly because you are anxious or distracted or in awe of your surroundings. It's easy to accidentally prioritize what's outside when you're engulfed in a whole new world that is shouting for your attention.[3]

In my everyday life, I can likewise fall into a pattern of getting absorbed in my environment and its inputs. I'll be the first to admit to immediately plopping down on the sofa to "relax" after work by putting on a TV show and simultaneously scrolling on my phone to catch up on all the chatter from the day. Sometimes when I'm using my phone, I'll even catch myself holding my breath—tech apnea.[4]

It's almost too easy to accidentally spend all day like this, losing myself to hours of consuming. Whether it's for work, or entertainment, or simply because I'm bored, I can find myself immersed in listening, watching, reading. It can be inspirational and educational and useful. Or it can be passive and dull. Either way, when there's too much inflow and not enough outflow, it's almost like I'm hyperventilating on information. I can feel it in my body.

So just as while diving, to maintain a type of on-land buoyancy, I've learned to become more attuned to my inner state (interoception) and mindful of how I'm taking in external stimuli (exteroception). The former can be as simple as resting, or taking a walk without tech, or starting to wind down earlier in the

---

3 Information overload is when there is just too much information in the world; we have no choice but to filter almost all of it out. Our brain uses a few simple tricks to pick out the bits of information that are most likely going to be useful in some way.

4 *Email apnea* was a term that the writer Linda Stone coined in 2008 when she noticed a temporary absence or suspension of breathing, or shallow breathing, while reading her emails.

night. The latter is more actively balancing the inputs with the outputs—making time for creating, drawing, imagining, and sharing (ISOLATED CHOICE EFFECT).

This cycle is meant to feel as natural as breathing: to inhale is akin to reading and listening, and to exhale is akin to speaking and writing. The exhalation—or the emptying—is crucial to this flow. By sharing and verbalizing, you digest the information and come up with coherent thoughts of your own. By making your thoughts tangible, you learn to find inconsistencies and assumptions in what you've learned. You add texture to your own intimate understanding (EFFORT JUSTIFICATION).

So the next time you find yourself holding your breath, take note. If there's too much information, try to stay buoyant and make meaning. The process can change you.

✳ BIASES TO EXPLORE

Attentional bias, pg 173:
If we think about something, we'll notice it more in our day-to-day.

Isolated choice effect, pg 233:
We tend to make decisions about our choices in isolation, without considering the larger context or the collective impact of our decisions on our goals.

Effort justification, pg 200:
When we work for something, we end up valuing it more. Some people also refer to this as the IKEA effect.

Mapo Tofu

+ **QUESTIONS**

- What's for lunch?
- How do I set financial goals and stick to them?
- Should I change my career path?
- Am I willing to take a pay cut to live a slower, more stress-free life?
- Am I taking enough time off?

I grew up a latchkey kid in the '90s, watching music videos on MTV after school, belly down on a sheepskin rug, waiting for my mom to get home. Every night after work, she would prepare simple Taiwanese home-cooked meals for dinner—lion's head meatballs with napa cabbage, saucy beef and tomato, black bean spare ribs, and mapo tofu, served over rice with sautéed leafy greens on the side.

The steady rotation of dishes was comforting. I'd see the ingredients marinating in green onion, ginger, and soy sauce in the morning and look forward to the savory smells wafting into the living room, signaling dinnertime. Sundays were special: pan-fried pork-and-chive dumplings made by a neighborhood lao tàitài, giving my mom a well-deserved rest day. These flavors shaped my palate in subtle and meaningful ways.

The comforting routines of my childhood felt worlds away as, decades later, I found myself working at a startup in sunny Los Angeles. In our company's spacious common area, on the expansive blue wall stretching above to the second floor, the big white letters of our lofty mission served as a reminder of our shared charter to improve the health and happiness of the world.

This position had been a dream job, but the motto had started to feel a bit arrogant. My days were spent designing digital experiences to encourage users to build healthy habits around a daily meditation routine. My interpretation of our mission was to help customers become self-sufficient in their practice—less technology allowing for more presence. However, the company's goals were to keep customers using their service, so they could keep earning subscription revenue in service of growing the company.

Most weeks I was able to compartmentalize this tension and tuck it away in a hidden corner of my mind. But every so often, there would be a decision that felt like a huge affront, causing the contents of that box to come spilling out. The day I quit, I could no longer bear the feeling of sacrificing my personal values for a paycheck.

In leaving, my intention was not simply to swap out one startup for another. I had sampled enough tech companies to understand that this was a systemic problem. Rather, my goal was to create a financially stable situation that would allow me to work in a sustainable way. This was about making a long-term lifestyle change.

To that end, I structured my time off around a budgeted amount of money rather than a fixed duration. This "exploration fund" was self-reinforcing, allowing me to earn more time if I found paying work I enjoyed doing, enabling a different type of lifestyle—an experiment to see if I could work and live the way I wanted.

There were a few categories of projects I planned to explore:

1. **Fun projects:** These were the wild ideas and pipe dreams I had tucked away over the years, unable to pursue them alongside the demands of my desk job. These projects allowed me to stretch and flex different muscles, like crafting with my hands and working with tangible, physical materials.
2. **Career-adjacent projects:** These were ideas that allowed me to use my existing skill set in alternative ways to working full time, such as advising smaller companies without funding or mentoring early stage or underrepresented designers. These projects could extend my "exploration fund" without sacrificing the first category.
3. **Values-aligned full-time job:** This was a safety net in case I exhausted all my other options. The goal was to find a position rooted in a value system that better aligned with my own.

During this period, I found myself cooking versions of mapo tofu and other Taiwanese dishes my mom had made for us. This simple routine of cooking familiar dishes became an unexpected anchor during my period of exploration and change. Making a trip to the Asian grocery store for fresh ingredients and preparing a simple meal became a weekly ritual. The familiar scent of ginger and garlic sizzling in the wok, the crunchy red chili oil swirling into the tofu—these sensory experiences grounded me in a time of uncertainty.

As the weeks went on, I realized this was also helping me simplify decision-making each day. It freed me from having to find new spots to try at lunchtime, a task that often led to indulgence and distraction, especially now that I wasn't spending my days in the office (ISOLATED CHOICE EFFECT). Having mapo tofu waiting for me at home also made it easier for me to eat healthy, portioned meals by default (RESTRAINT BIAS).

In this larger moment, when I had changed so much about my routine—where I work, who I see each day, what I spend my days thinking about—it was a welcome thread of stability. My simple Taiwanese lunch box sitting ready in the fridge reminded me of the work I intended to accomplish that week.

In this way, mapo tofu helped me move into a default money-saving mode. It wasn't about not eating out; it just made more sense to eat in. The comfort and nostalgia of the meal, the return to the simple flavors of my childhood, made it easy to look forward to eating at home. The cost savings, in turn, contributed in small ways to the foundation of the larger lifestyle change as I was exploring this new way of working (DENOMINATION EFFECT).

For me, the simple act of cooking my childhood meals became a powerful tool in reshaping my life and career. It provided comfort, reduced decision fatigue, and contributed to my financial goals, all while connecting me to my roots. This experience has shown me the profound impact that small, intentional changes can have on achieving larger life goals.

What small, comforting rituals can you incorporate into your own pursuit of a larger goal? Like cooking mapo tofu, these rituals could be just what you need to make the changes feel more attainable and sustainable.

✳ BIASES TO EXPLORE

Isolated choice effect, pg 233:

We tend to make decisions about our choices in isolation, without considering the larger context or the collective impact of our decisions on our goals.

Restraint bias, pg 257:

We think we're better at resisting temptations than we are.

Denomination effect, pg 194:

We're less likely to spend large denominations than small ones, even if the amount is the same.

Yancey's Mustache

+ **QUESTIONS**

- How can I stop procrastinating?
- How can I improve my self-esteem and confidence?
- How can I be more motivated?

Tapping into a hidden self to overcome doubt. This intriguing strategy stuck with me after a chance encounter with Yancey Strickler, cofounder of the creative crowdfunding platform Kickstarter.

At an "experimental event" in Los Angeles—a trial run for concepts from Yancey's upcoming book, *This Could Be Our Future*—I learned about this creative approach for overcoming self-doubt.

While writing this book, Yancey felt the same doubt and insecurity that many of us feel when attempting an aspirational project that's just outside our comfort zone. As someone who has struggled with imposter syndrome myself, I found his vulnerability reassuring.[5] Even though Yancey felt competent and successful in many other aspects of his life, writing such an optimistic book about how to change the world felt daunting in a different way, and the pressure weighed heavily on him.

To overcome his feeling of stuck-ness, Yancey employed a

---

5 Impostor syndrome is a psychological occurrence in which we doubt our skills, talents, or accomplishments and have a fear of being exposed as frauds. Despite evidence of our competence, we find it difficult to believe we deserve our success or luck.

role-playing strategy that I love for its simplicity—he grew a mustache.

In mustachioed Yancey's words:

The clean-shaven, good-guy version of me struggled to express the bold ideas the book demanded. But somehow I was certain that the person who could, had a mustache. Someone too busy scheming to worry about what anybody else thought. I had to trick myself into becoming that person, and a mustache was the vehicle. As the mustache grew so did my confidence. My old fears faded and a new outlook took their place. (DUNNING-KRUGER EFFECT)

Yancey's trick was to "act out" the person he wanted to be until he became that person. This approach has a strong resemblance to Method acting, an approach developed by Konstantin Stanislavski, whose process of embodiment would push an actor into various emotional states, helping them become the characters they were playing. Method actors ask themselves, "What would motivate me, the actor, to behave in the way the character does? How would I behave, what would I do, how would I feel, how would I react?" (AFFECTIVE FORECASTING).

This idea of embodying a different version of ourselves isn't limited to writing books. The Beatles used it when "taking on the personas of a different band" and developing alter egos, as Paul McCartney described. Transforming themselves allowed them to leave behind the pressure of being the group that everyone already knew, which enabled them to experience the freedom of being a wholly different band. The result? Sgt. Pepper's Lonely Hearts Club Band.

We can apply this strategy in our everyday lives too. Think about how you might put on a power suit to feel more confident in a job interview, or adopt a "fake it till you make it" attitude when learning a new skill.

So, what happens when we apply these Method acting questions to our own lives? By asking ourselves what would motivate us and how we'd behave as our ideal selves, we can become the character we want to be in our future. Your transformation and embodiment might just be waiting for you within a pair of statement glasses or a bold new haircut.

✳ BIASES TO EXPLORE

Dunning-Kruger effect, pg 197:
When those of us who lack skill or knowledge tend to overestimate our abilities, and those of us with more knowledge or skill tend to underestimate them.

Affective forecasting, pg 158:
When we try to predict how we'll feel about something in the future, we tend to overestimate both the intensity and duration of our emotional reactions.

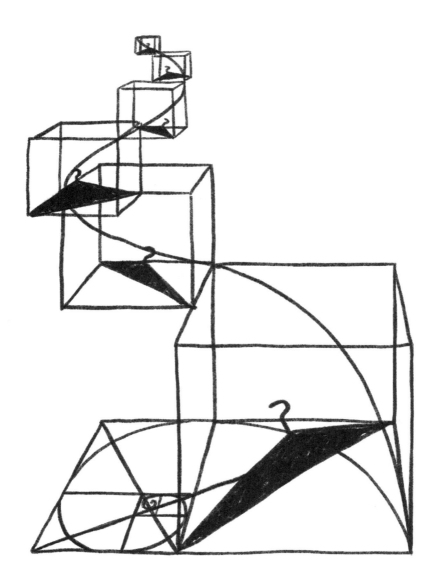

Hanger Math

+ **QUESTIONS**

- What should I wear today?
- How can I be more intentional in what I buy?
- Am I spending too much money?

In my closet, there are forty or so nice wooden hangers, and they all match. At one point during the growing-up cycle of moving, packing, purging, and nesting, I made a personally significant gesture to get rid of all my cheap plastic hangers, the wire dry-cleaning hangers, and the other odds-and-ends hangers that had accumulated over the years, and bought myself two sets of wooden hangers. After I had hung my articles of clothing, one by one, I found it satisfying to look into my closet. Everything was lined up, neatly organized, with my new hangers purposefully holding each garment just right.

At the end of this cathartic tidying, there were some remaining items of clothing that hadn't gotten the high honor of being selected for a hanger. I noticed that they were all things I didn't wear much but had schlepped from apartment to apartment because I had spent money on them (ENDOWMENT EFFECT). I hesitated to get rid of them because I didn't want to waste money, lest they fit well or come back into style or look good on me *someday*. But keeping them in my closet wouldn't justify my purchase (SUNK COST FALLACY). So I went through a ritual of wearing each item one last time and used the feeling I got to decide whether to keep them. The result was a slimmed-down closet of items that I loved and wore a lot.

This purging process led me to an important realization. Over decades of having to get dressed, buy clothes, and develop a point of view on style, I've noticed that I've become something of a "uniform gal," or someone who wears the same idiosyncratic piece for years. Call me a creature of habit. Sometimes I look at photos of myself and laugh that I'm wearing the same black jumpsuit that I was really into for nearly a decade! Like the traveling gnome from *Amélie*, this jumpsuit became my unlikely companion, accompanying me all around the world, showing up in photos and at events, and was once left in an Airbnb closet, eventually returned by a gracious host.

I've found that I love having my go-to items—pieces that are easy to wear but unique, that fit me well and help me feel confident, and that I can wear more days than not, with different tops, layers, and shoes. There's something so satisfying about a well-made garment that you can turn to again and again.

As I've shifted to this uniform mode, I've allowed myself to buy fewer but higher-quality clothes. Now, before making a purchase, I ask myself whether I can see myself wearing a potential purchase for years to come. How does this piece pair with the other items I already love? Do I already have something that is similar in look or function? And is there something already in my closet that I'm not wearing as much, that I'd be willing to let go of, to make hanger space for something new?

You might be wondering: Why not just buy more hangers? I could, but then my purchasing wouldn't have a self-limiting aspect. By rewarding the letting go of one garment when embracing another, you allow yourself to feel good about the purchase (SELF-LICENSING EFFECT). With hanger math, you can bring the cost per wear down, because you're holding yourself to a high purchase standard and using items frequently. Not only is this good for the environment, but it's also good for your wallet.

For those of you who aren't constantly tempted to buy clothes, you might apply this self-limiting system to any other consumer good you splurge on. Here are a few ways to apply this concept to other areas:

- **Books:** *Tsundoku* is the Japanese word for the stack of books you own but haven't yet read. I like to think of this as a humble stack of future knowledge and inspiration. While it's important to remind ourselves of what we don't know (DUNNING-KRUGER EFFECT), it can be easy to let this stack go unnoticed and keep buying more. If you can keep this pile to a list you can recite from memory—for many, the magical number is seven—it will keep the anticipation of reading front of mind (MAGICAL NUMBER 7±2).

- **Collections:** If you're a collector of baseball cards, rare coins, figurines, or anything else, dedicate a shelf or a case to display your collection. Ask yourself what you value in this act of collecting and compare it to what you value in seeing the collection.

- **Electronics/appliances:** Getting new electronics or appliances can be tempting because their purchase feels justified by their utility (POST-PURCHASE RATIONALIZATION). The thinking tends to go, "Once I have this new *thing*—the latest AirPods, an air fryer, or a fitness tracker—I will be so much more productive at work, experiment with healthy dishes, or be motivated to exercise more." While these tools might provide an external nudge in some situations, before you buy, check whether you already have something that does this job for you today. Challenge yourself to accomplish this task with the existing tool, and reward yourself with the upgrade afterward if you still want it.

✳ BIASES TO EXPLORE

Endowment effect, pg 203:
We value things that we own more than what we don't, regardless of the real value of the items.

Sunk cost fallacy, pg 266:
The more we invest in something, the harder it becomes to abandon it.

Self-licensing effect, pg 260:
We give ourselves permission to do things we consider "bad" after we've done things we consider "good."

Dunning-Kruger effect, pg 197:

When those of us who lack skill or knowledge tend to overestimate our abilities, and those of us with more knowledge or skill tend to underestimate them.

Magical number 7±2:

The number of objects the average mind can hold at once in working memory is seven, plus or minus two.

Post-purchase rationalization, pg 251:

When we buy something, we tend to value it more after the fact.

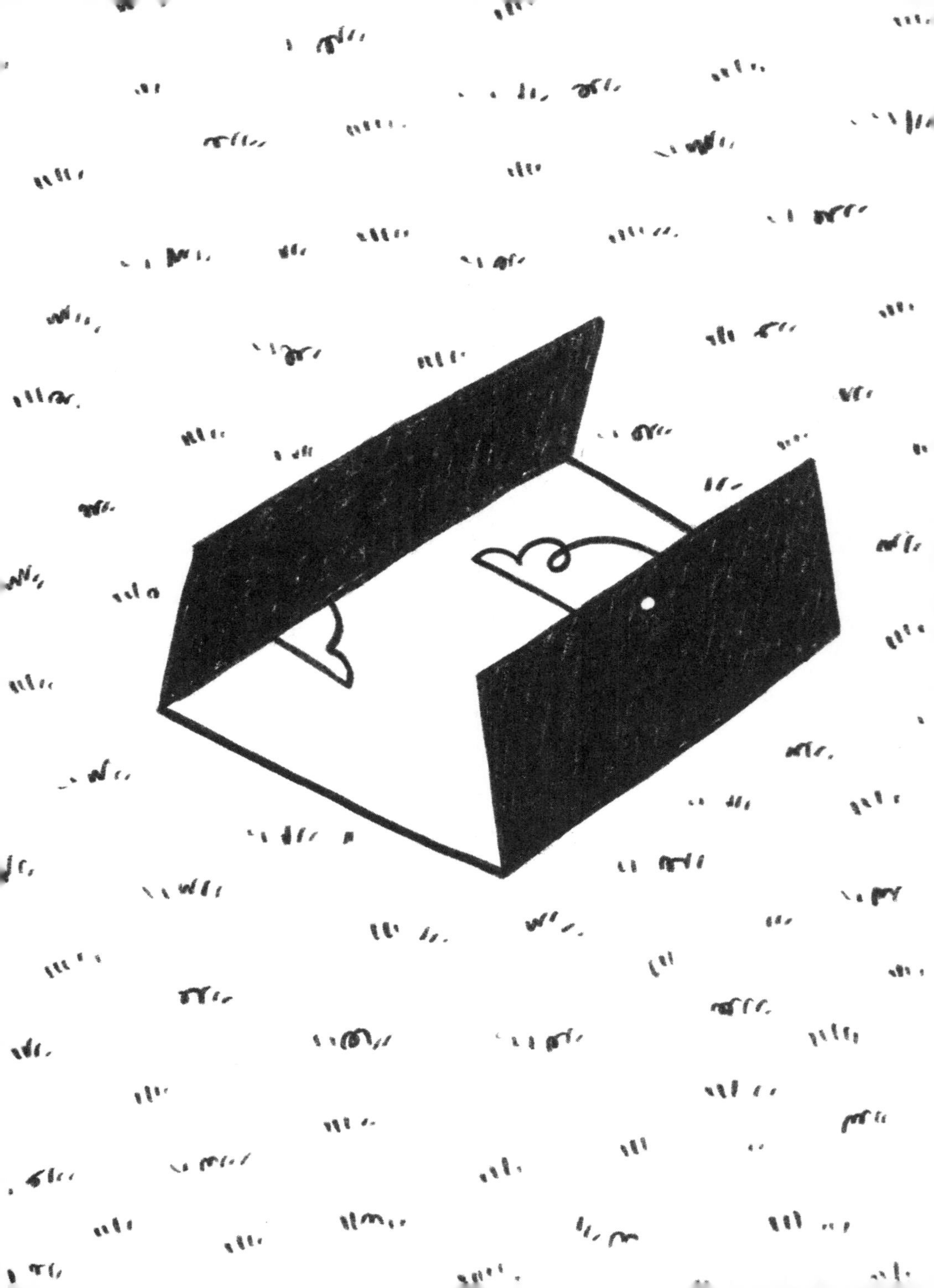

Trim Grass

+ QUESTIONS

- What do I want right now?
- How can I stop overthinking or ruminating?
- How do I deal with emotions like anger, fear, anxiety, and sadness?
- How can I become inspired?
- How can I have a healthy relationship with social media?
- How can I make travel more personally meaningful?
- What do I do when I'm feeling stuck?

The wet grass clung to Andy's fingers as he methodically trimmed the vast monastery lawn, one blade at a time. The absurdity of the task before him—cutting a field the size of three tennis courts with a pair of scissors—was not lost on him. As the sun climbed higher in the sky, warming his back, Andy's initial fury began to cool, replaced by an unexpected sense of peace.

This scene, from one of Andy's most memorable stories, has always stuck in my mind. It was shared during one of the weekly dharma talks at the meditation company where I worked. My favorite part of the job was hearing Andy, one of our founders and a former Tibetan monk, share these talks.

They were a common ritual in monasteries, and it felt like going to a mini-lecture each week about meditation. Andy would typically share a personal story that would have a lesson contained within, and afterward we could ask questions that had come up about our mindfulness practice.

This particular story began with Andy getting into trouble at the monastery. As punishment, he was given the task of cutting all the grass on the grounds. But when Andy went to get the lawn mower from the shed, an elder monk handed him a pair of scissors and instructed him, in a stern tone, to use those instead.

Flabbergasted, Andy laughed at the suggestion and questioned how the heck he was supposed to trim such a big lawn in this way. The elder chastised him for speaking to an elder in that manner and told him that's what he had to do. Infuriated and fuming with resentment, Andy knelt down in the wet grass and started trimming it. Blade by blade, as you might trim someone's hair.

As Andy methodically cut each blade, his mind began to clear. The constant chatter of his thoughts slowed. With each snip, he found himself more present, more grounded in the physical world around him.

Nowadays, there is a saying that internet people say to other internet people when it seems like they've been online for too long. When their behavior, whether it be an unhinged social media blowout or assuming a myopic point of view, indicates they've lost touch with reality. It's kind of an insult and tongue-in-cheek advice smushed into one: "Touch grass." Meaning, you should log off and get outside. Sometimes they skip the phrase altogether and just send an image of grass.

Perhaps it's more of an insult, because a scrap of lawn is the most suburban, minimally viable bit of the earthy outdoors. To suggest that you might emerge from your bedroom and venture out past the front door and onto the lawn is in contrast to how far you truly are from actually being outdoors, among lush redwoods or on a mossy mountaintop.

But "Touch grass" kind of works because grass is . . . everywhere. And if you read about agrostology, the branch of botany dedicated to grasses, you'll quickly learn that they are very important plants to us. In addition to being a nice thing to sit and play on, we eat a ton of grasses in the form of rice, wheat, and maize (corn). We eat animals that eat grasses. By the law of the transitive property, you might even say that we, too, are grass.

The moral of Andy's story was that he had trapped himself within his own frustration and anger. And once he was able to laugh at the absurdity of it, he could let go of the idea that it was unfair. Suddenly, he was released from the tension of the story he had created in his mind. And after that, in his telling, it became a pleasant experience.

To me, this is how it feels to be online these days. We find ourselves spending hours on irresistible platforms that give us tunnel vision. In turn, this digital reality clouds our physical reality. For someone in my age group, it's seeing my friends at beautifully curated weddings, on picturesque European vacations, and hosting idyllic first birthdays.

I see influencers that I identify with sharing makeup tutorials, morning monologues, and positive affirmations about how I can live my fullest life. These clever algorithms make it easy for us to connect with those who we strongly identify with, sometimes aspirationally, but in doing so, it can become harder to grasp our own individuality (IN-GROUP BIAS).

The risks of this casual internet usage are in the subtle shifts that happen over time. No one is going to tell you to touch grass for scrolling through your feed when you're bored. But on your next vacation, rather than wandering the city in a mode of discovery, you might find yourself checking off the places you saw on an influencer's itinerary. The thrill of stumbling upon hidden gems and crafting your own unique adventures is replaced by a prepackaged, curated experience that aligns with someone else's vision of the perfect trip. Or perhaps you're scrolling through your feed, seeing couples sharing their most romantic, Instagrammable moment, and you start to wonder if you're missing out on some key ingredient for long-term happiness, if you're settling for something less than perfect.

And in time, you feel a dissonance because you are constantly and subconsciously comparing your life to the milestones of others and a culture that you never chose. Your life is filled with beautiful moments of your own qualia, yet you inexplicably feel like you're falling behind.

Could it be that being *a little bit* online has shifted your internal view of all the ways that your life is already enough (CLUSTERING ILLUSION)?

Social media is designed to grab our attention by showcasing the most enviable aspects of people's lives. By pulling us into these highlight reels, it can cause us to lose sight of our own unique paths. We might not even realize how these curated glimpses are shaping our expectations and desires, subtly eroding our sense of contentment.

Back to the grass for a moment.

The reason why we have to mow lawns at all is because grass has a low meristem, the part that's responsible for keeping the plant growing. These cells are similar to stem cells in humans—

they are the magical life-giving cells that have the potential to develop into all the other tissues and organs that we need to live.

Because grass has a meristem that is close to the ground, it can avoid the blades of lawn mowers and grazing animals. We can trim down the growth and the meristem will spring fresh length anew each week. While you might have objections to lawns (as we do in California), it's easy to find a patch almost anywhere.

The next time you feel your mind getting sucked into the internet vortex, remember: we are grass and we, too, have a meristem. We have the innate capacity for growth and resilience, even when faced with constant external influences. To reconnect with this resilience, ask yourself: What task in your life are you resisting, and how might embracing it unexpectedly cultivate your growth?

✳ BIASES TO EXPLORE

In-group bias, pg 230:
We favor members of groups we belong to (the in-groups) over members of groups we don't (the out-groups).

Clustering illusion, pg 188:
We tend to see clusters and streaks in data that aren't really there.

Hsu Ken's Dad

+ QUESTIONS

- How can I have more structure but not have to follow so many rules for myself?
- How can I create an environment that allows my children to thrive?
- How can I become financially secure?
- How do I become adaptable in my work?
- How can I be more intentional with what I learn?
- How can I be more patient?

I've always admired my friend Hsu Ken for his approachable intelligence—his ability to explain complex ideas with remarkable simplicity. Our paths crossed during a pivotal moment in my career when I was hesitating to leave a secure job and a great company for something unknown. Through patient guidance, Hsu Ken taught me the art of quitting with purpose and confidence.[6]

What fascinates me most about Hsu Ken is his unconventional career path. Unlike me, who had always worked for others, Hsu Ken had never held a traditional job. What led him to break out of the typical working cycle that everyone else had obligingly opted into? There were likely many factors—his personality, the decade he was born in, and of course, luck. But the

---

6 See *Good at Quitting*, pg 107.

roots of his entrepreneurial spirit, I discovered, were nurtured by a unique source: his father's approach to birthday gifts.

Hsu Ken's family story is one of immigrant determination and financial wisdom. His parents came from modest beginnings in Malaysia and prioritized stability for their family after moving to the United States. When his dad took a role at Intel in 1978, in the early days before they started making central processing units (CPUs) for computers, he had chosen it purely for its high salary. Decades of diligent work led to promotions, slowly rising through the ranks, and, unknowingly, a growing stock portfolio.

The turning point came with an unexpected call from a brokerage firm holding his stock options, asking him what he wanted to do with his money. "What money?" he asked. His stock options turned out to be much more than he had ever made from his salary. He experienced an epiphany and dove into learning about the stock market, quickly grasping how wealth truly accumulates. And as Hsu Ken put it, he quickly learned that this is how rich people got rich.

With this newfound knowledge about stocks and how they compound year over year, he understood that he should have started doing this much earlier. This sparked an innovative idea. He called in his two sons, Hsu Ken and his brother, Hsu Han, aged ten and nine at the time, and announced a change in birthday traditions—instead of toys, they would receive one hundred shares of a stock of their choice. The only catch was that Hsu Ken and his brother would have to explain why they wanted to buy that particular stock.

Initially disappointed at hearing "no presents," the two boys felt ripped off. What the heck was a stock anyway? They wanted toys like everyone else. Yet they were inquisitive enough to ask their dad, "What's so good about a stock?"

Their father's response was simple yet profound: "You can buy a bike today, but if you buy a stock, you can buy two bikes and more next year" (TIME DISCOUNTING). This lesson in delayed gratification and compound growth would shape their financial mindset for years to come.

Over the years, this unconventional birthday gift evolved into a shared passion, forging a unique bond between them. Their dad's approach was always inquisitive: asking questions back to the boys, fostering dialogue, guiding them to think critically about their choices. This early exposure to investing did more than build financial literacy; it instilled a confidence in making informed decisions and taking calculated risks (MERE EXPOSURE EFFECT).

The true value of this education became clear when Hsu Ken graduated college. Supported with the knowledge and safety net of his stock portfolio, he took the bold step of starting his own company. The financial cushion from his birthday-gifted stocks allowed him to weather the lean early years of entrepreneurship—a luxury many new graduates don't have.

Today, Hsu Ken's success as a startup investor—providing funding, mentorship, and resources to others—stands as a testament to his father's enduring influence. He attributes his entrepreneurial success not just to the financial benefits of his dad's unorthodox birthday gifts, but also to the mindset they fostered, which has shaped his entire career (EFFORT JUSTIFICATION). Just as his father's initiative to learn about stocks set Hsu Ken and his brother on a path to success, Hsu Ken's influence inspired me to find the courage to make my own career change.

While we can't retroactively create this arrangement for ourselves (if only!), Hsu Ken's story offers valuable lessons about the power of experiential learning and long-term thinking. We can create our own opportunities by:

1. Joining groups that expose us to new ideas, such as a book club exploring unfamiliar genres. The group's momentum and accountability can push us to broaden our literary horizons.
2. Engaging in monthly challenges that expand our boundaries, like trying a new recipe every week. Often, the simple nudge of a suggestion gets the hardest step out of the way. As the challenge goes on, we develop muscle memory and fluency in routines.

Remember, experiential learning isn't confined to structured activities or career changes. The key is to let your curiosity be your guide and remain open to the learning opportunities that come with each new experience (AMBIGUITY EFFECT).

Hsu Ken's story reminds us that the most valuable gifts often aren't tangible objects, but the tools and mindsets that enable us to shape our own futures. Whether it's through unconventional birthday presents or self-imposed challenges, personal growth stems from embracing the unfamiliar and being willing to learn.

✳ BIASES TO EXPLORE

Time discounting:
We value things in the present more than things in the future. A type of **affective forecasting, pg 158**.

Mere exposure effect:
We tend to develop a preference for things merely because we are familiar with them. This is one way things like advertising can influence us, by repeating a message that we don't agree with but become familiar with.

Effort justification, pg 200:
When we work for something, we end up valuing it more. Some people also refer to this as the IKEA effect.

Ambiguity effect, pg 161:
We choose options that are more certain, even if those options are likely to be worse.

Trees

+ QUESTIONS

- How do I find my path in life?
- How can I improve my self-esteem and confidence?
- How do I find my life's purpose or calling?
- How do I face my biggest fears?

When I signed up for a continuing education course at a local university, I felt excited at the prospect of becoming a better public speaker.

Yet there I was, sitting in the familiar stadium-style seats of a massive lecture hall feeling only . . . nausea. It was the first day of class and the professor had just handed out prompts for a warm-up exercise. My slip of paper simply read: *trees*. I stared at it with my heart racing, palms clammy, and legs imperceptibly shaking.

How was I going to get up there to talk about *trees*?

Thinking back on this moment, I'm a little dumbfounded by my reaction. Not because I don't know about glossophobia, or the irrational fear of public speaking. But because I know myself to be a social, outgoing person who is comfortable speaking in groups. I also revel in the thrill of an adventure. I've even been called an adrenaline junkie because I enjoy riding motorcycles, rock climbing, and scuba diving. These activities feel freeing and exploratory, full-body experiences that help me experience flow states. I gravitate toward all-consuming experiences that might give others pause.

Yet in that moment, I was in a state of panic, frantically jotting down gibberish about trees. Leaves. Chlorophyll. Root systems. Gravitropism. Oldest organisms ever. It wasn't that I couldn't think of anything to say about trees. It was that the act of vocalizing coherent sentences in front of that classroom felt physically impossible. I started scheming escape plans. I thought about feigning sickness. I actually *did* feel sick. Could I pull off saying that I had a family emergency? That might be bad luck. Maybe I would accidentally trip on the way down to the front of the room and twist an ankle. I fantasized about evaporating. Could I channel sublimation? My mind had uncontrollably shifted to flight mode and was flooded with nonsensical ideas. Without warning, I abruptly stood up. I walked out with no explanation. I never returned.

In the weeks after, I felt an unexplainable but extreme sense of shame. I didn't tell any of my friends or family that I had abandoned class midway through the first day. The thought of admitting my cowardice made my stomach churn.

Once the panic had subsided to a lower-grade embarrassment, I felt something shift. The part of me that had been able to ignore this fear had dislodged and was now unavoidable, like a splinter working its way to the surface. I made a tiny internal commitment to myself. Fix it, get better, and do something so that I never had to experience that paralysis again.

In the years that followed, I changed careers from academia to tech and discovered the many extracurriculars and employee benefits tech had to offer. Among these, I found Toastmasters, a program for improving public speaking through group practice. Hoping that practicing with peers in an informal setting would be more comfortable (AMBIGUITY EFFECT), I signed up. Yet I finished that year never having mustered the courage to attend a single session. That feeling from the classroom lingered persistently, like a barnacle on my gut.

As I started to transition to a design career, I found myself sharing my experiences on Medium to a small but engaged audience. As I gained more experience in different types of companies, I began to find my niche as a designer, understanding which aspects of my nontraditional path were relatable and useful in this field.

In 2018, I got my first real public-speaking opportunity to a big audience on a proper stage. The Eccles Theater in Salt Lake City seats twenty-five hundred with orchestra, mezzanine, and balcony sections. I would be on a stage that Broadway performers and opera singers had stood on. And despite the scale and stakes, I felt ready, excited, and not anxious at the prospect of speaking onstage.

I was fastidious in how I spent the months before the event, practicing, seeking feedback, diligently editing, improving my inflection, and getting the timing down. When the day came, everything was a success and a blur. Afterward I learned that my talk was the audience favorite and in the years to follow had become one of the conference's most-viewed talks on YouTube.

In the end, the key in overcoming my fear was not the obvious solution: practicing public speaking (AVAILABILITY BIAS).

Or trying to mimic the path of accomplished designers that I looked up to (SURVIVORSHIP BIAS). Instead, it turned out to be a more subtle and indirect approach that involved discovering ways of growing that felt safe and approachable.

As I stood backstage behind the theater drapes, I could hear the low murmur of the audience and feel the vibration of my heartbeat. But this time, it wasn't panic—it was excitement. The smell of the stage, a mix of wood and heavy velour, filled my nostrils. I took a deep breath, feeling the cool air fill my lungs.

Those small, consistent actions over the years had helped me chip away at that old barnacle of fear, moving past the deeper emotional crux to a place where I felt at ease. As I stepped onto the stage, the bright lights warm on my face, I realized that in finding my voice, my audience, and what I wanted to say as a public speaker, I had discovered a quiet confidence within myself that felt true to me.

✳ BIASES TO EXPLORE

Ambiguity effect, pg 161:
We choose options that are more certain, even if those options are likely to be worse.

Availability bias, pg 176:
We tend to favor the options that come to mind easily. Things that don't, for whatever reason, are at a severe disadvantage.

Survivorship bias, pg 269:
When we try to figure out the cause of success, we look at people or solutions that have succeeded but forget to consider those that have failed.

Memory-Foam Pillow

+ **QUESTIONS**

- How can I be more courageous?
- How can I create environments where I thrive?
- How can I trust in myself?

Much to the chagrin of my current self, my younger twentysomething, too-cool-to-care self spent most of her college years and beyond avoiding travel. While most of my friends were jumping at the chance to go abroad for life-enriching programs, I was content to spend my summers in sunny San Diego, riding my fixed-gear bike around town and deferring any thinking about my future career.

It wasn't that I disliked beautiful places and the adventures that might await—in theory, I loved all that. My qualm was more of an annoying "me" problem. I'm a light sleeper. (If I have a superpower, it is the useless ability to hear even the tiniest noise while asleep—a door creaking or a car driving by on the street will jolt me awake.)

Consequently, I can't sleep on flights. I arrive at destinations jet-lagged, and when I'm finally horizontal, there's always a lumpy mattress I can rely on to keep me tossing and turning. Travel just didn't feel worth it!

That's the thing with us humans. When it comes to our emotions, we tend to assume that we'll feel a certain way in the future, based on how we feel *in the moment*. Our current self attempts to "forecast" our feelings so our future self will be prepared. It's a thoughtful thing we do for ourselves, but we tend to be incorrect when it comes to stress and anxiety.

In reality, our body has a whole bunch of coping strategies that it uses in the moment to make things easier to deal with (AFFECTIVE FORECASTING). These predictions can cause us to avoid all sorts of uncomfortable things in our lives that could be quite wonderful (like travel!) if we could just get to the other side of whatever feels so daunting.

Eventually, I left the slow, nest-like pace of Southern California and joined the adult world. I started working for a company in a role that required some travel. It was on that team that I met Alex—a suave, likable, extroverted type who seemed to thrive on new experiences. He and I were on the far ends of the same team at work: he on the recruiting side, and I on the research side, developing a framework for hiring. Our paths converged when we got sent on a trip to our Asia-Pacific offices to train our teams to use this new framework.

While I was eager to see our offices in Singapore, Malaysia, and Indonesia, I was also bracing for an uncomfortable trip. I was so anxious about getting there and being able to sleep enough to be functional that I could hardly imagine embracing the adventure. Alex, on the other hand, had cheerily volunteered. A gregarious traveler, he didn't seem to have a single worry about the logistics of this multicountry trip that I was fretting over.

The day came, and almost as if I had manifested it, our long-haul flight out of San Francisco was delayed. When we landed for our layover, we had to rush through a massive airport terminal to find our connecting flight. With the gate finally in sight, I was dismayed to see that a long line had formed at passport control. Before I'd even had a chance to register defeat, Alex walked to the front of the line without skipping a beat and explained our predicament. And voilà! I settled into my seat feeling like someone had just told me a secret. I was so impressed by Alex simply asking for what we needed—and then getting it! It was intoxicating. I felt enthralled at the prospect of one day having the confidence to do it myself.

As corporate travel goes, we spent our trip bopping around from hotel to hotel. To my surprise, I found myself enjoying sleeping on luxurious, high-thread-count sheets that were, dare I say, *better* than my digs at home. While it might sound obvious to anyone with the means to afford it, this was my first time experiencing a trip abroad where the sleep could be *better* than what I was used to. Even though it was a tiring trip, it also felt worthwhile and fulfilling.

Things started to change from there, but in this slow, landslide sort of way.

While I still mostly couldn't afford fancy hotels, I discovered that I could make special accommodations for my travel concerns. When I learned how to add comfort where discomfort was anticipated, it was like a magic door opened for me! I started bringing my own pillow on trips. Initially, the idea of lugging a pillow around was embarrassing because it felt childish, conjuring up memories of summer camp and sleepovers. My pillow of choice was made of heavy memory foam and took up a lot of space in my luggage. Despite the bulk, I decided the comfort was worth the effort.

But here's the other thing. We tend to adjust our behavior

based on how risky or scary we think a situation is. If it's risky, we will act more cautiously. And if we feel safer, we will be more tolerant—even reckless! Think about how helmets and seat-belts give us a sense of security. If I could look past how much I disliked bringing my memory-foam pillow along, could it safe-guard me against an anticipated bad night of sleep (RISK COM-PENSATION)?

In those moments when I felt even a small bit of pillow shame sneaking in, I remembered to channel my inner Alex, reaching for his self-assured confidence in knowing what I need and not feeling bad about it, however silly it looked. Lo and behold, the more trips I went on, the less apprehensive I became of having to bring extra items or make special requests (WELL-TRAVELED ROAD EFFECT). The ability to open myself to possibilities and understand myself in a new way created a sensation of power.

These days, I don't take my pillow with me anymore. But I do bring noise-canceling headphones and earplugs, and that gets me most of the way to comfort.

Looking back, I hardly recognize the reluctant traveler I once was. The person who dreaded sleeping away from her safe bed haven had transformed into an adventurer who embarked on a cross-country motorcycle ride with no itinerary![7] My for-mer self would have been shocked to see me taking long-haul flights with ease, striking up conversations with strangers, and waking up each morning to the unfamiliar sounds of bustling foreign cities.

---

7 See *Invariables*, pg 139.

I never told Alex that our trip showed me how to travel fear-lessly. But once I saw it, I couldn't let it go. What are some things that you may be avoiding because you're anticipating they will be unpleasant? Think about what makes the experience challenging for you and if there are ways that you can create safety for yourself.

✳ BIASES TO EXPLORE

Affective forecasting, pg 158:
When we try to predict how we'll feel about something in the future, we tend to overestimate both the intensity and duration of our emotional reactions.

Risk compensation:
A theory that suggests we adjust our behavior based on the perceived level of risk. We are more careful when we sense greater risk and less careful when we feel more protected. This leads to an overall reduction in the effectiveness of added safety measures, since we compensate by becoming a bit more reckless.

Well-traveled road effect:
We estimate that travel time on frequently traveled routes will be less than our estimates of traveling on unfamiliar routes, even if they're the same distance.

Slow Shopping

+ **QUESTIONS**

- How can I be less impulsive?
- Should I make this big purchase?
- How can I create environments where I thrive?

"Buy it right, or buy it twice." A carpenter friend used to recite this mantra as a lesson about buying quality tools that would last a lifetime. His experience was that if you skimped and bought the cheap tool, it would break sooner rather than later, so you might as well buy the good one (RHYME AS REASON EFFECT).

Being a woodworker, he naturally extended this philosophy to furniture. He was always on the hunt for lost treasures, often midcentury modern–designed pieces made of solid walnut and teak. I loved watching him score treasures found tucked away in old garages and at estate sales, the musty scent of old wood and memories filling the air. In his shop, I watched the wood take on a new life as he refinished it, using finer and finer grains of sandpaper to wipe away years of use. The final step, a layer of Danish oil, and the piece was reborn, its smooth surface inviting to the touch.

Buying furniture feels more challenging than some other adult purchases because it costs a lot more and we don't get much practice at it. We usually do it once, on the cheap, if we move away to college, and then in bits and pieces in our twenties in the form of small upgrades to our bedding, plants, and kitchenware. Furniture falls squarely in the vast gray area between your everyday purchases and buying a home, on financial par with a vacation or leasing a car. And unlike a holiday away, we have to literally live with it.

Over the years, I've developed my own method of shopping for furniture (and other large purchases) that carries the essence of "buy it right, or buy it twice": use your personal style as a compass for the pieces you really want, and then shop slowly, as if you're on a treasure hunt.

The first step is all about understanding what feels the most right for *you*. Seek something that reflects your personality, suits your functional needs, and just makes you excited to own. When you're ready to buy, remember that "buying it right" isn't necessarily about spending the most money. Instead, it's about finding that perfect sofa that not only matches your aesthetic but also has you looking forward to sinking into it at the end of a long day. Once you know what you're looking for, affordability can fall into place more naturally.

The next step is to take it slow. There are many reasons why we buy things in a hurry. We might be overwhelmed by choice and just want to get it over with. Or maybe we are feeling aspirational and think this purchase will help us become the future person we want to be. We might be revenge spending after a long day in the office, indulging in retail therapy to offset existential work frustration. Any of these influences might be causing you to shop in a hurried and impulsive way, not enjoying the process and not loving what you end up with. Shopping slowly gives you time to anticipate owning something, which can increase your subjective enjoyment of it (POST-PURCHASE RATIONALIZATION).

Being patient with your timeline also creates a bigger window of opportunity to find the piece you want at the price you want it. When you wait to buy, you can access seasonal sales, compare prices online, and find treasures at estate sales or thrift shops.

Shopping in this way can feel exciting, like an adventure. If you don't find a deal, it's perfectly fine to buy Your Dream Sofa from the store where you found it, at the full price. The trick is that if you don't really want it, the temporal window and the chase for a better price give you time to change your mind. But if you truly love the piece, you increase your chances of saving money *and* being satisfied. It's a way to check in with yourself about your commitment.

While it might take more time and investment upfront to shop this way, learning to enjoy the process of researching and cultivating your home can be satisfying in the long term (HYPERBOLIC DISCOUNTING). In time, your home will start to evolve into a place where each object has meaning and intentionality, creating a cohesive vision. And when your home is filled with objects you love, you might even find yourself creating a routine of cleaning and caring for them in a new way.

✳ BIASES TO EXPLORE

Rhyme as reason effect:
We tend to believe that rhyming statements are more meaningful or accurate or truthful than those that don't rhyme.

Post-purchase rationalization, pg 251:
When we buy something, we tend to value it more after the fact.

Hyperbolic discounting, pg 221:
We tend to value things that pay off immediately over things that pay off in the future.

Airport Optimism

+ **QUESTIONS**

- How can I be more considerate of others?
- How can I be more prepared for the future?

A controversial topic in every one of my relationships to date has been how early we should arrive at the airport before our flight. Airlines generally suggest two hours for domestic flights and three hours for international flights. This has always felt way too early for me, so I prefer to arrive at the airport with the exact amount of time necessary to breeze through Pre-Check and board after everyone has been seated (ILLUSION OF CONTROL).

In contrast, nearly all of my partners have preferred arriving early. They were perfectly content to sit and wait around for hours at the airport. They would rather have the extra time buffer for unforeseen delays. This preparedness gave them a sense of calm, whereas my approach elicited extreme anxiety, especially if we got stuck in traffic on the way to the airport or encountered another obstacle. I consider myself optimistic (OPTIMISM BIAS), while they consider themselves prepared.

Even though these days I do arrive a bit earlier, I share this example to illustrate a broader point: our tendency to underestimate catastrophe can show up anywhere—in airports, yes, but also in more critical situations like wildfires, pandemics, and climate change. And if you're like me and you're inclined to believe everything will be all right, it's hard to motivate yourself to prepare for disaster (NORMALCY BIAS). Whether we're talking about airport arrival times, public health precautions, or emergency preparedness, it can be helpful to think about our options through the lens of highest cost or risk to ourselves and those around us.

For example, if I plan to arrive early at the airport, the worst that might happen is that I'm bored or tired because I had to wake up a couple of hours earlier. If I don't arrive early and there are unexpected issues, the biggest risk is that I could miss my flight, have to pay to rebook a flight, and ruin vacation plans for everyone involved. This might sound obvious, but it's helpful to list and compare the costs that could happen as a result of not being prepared for something to go wrong. The risk is clearly higher for the latter.

Similarly, during the first year of the COVID-19 pandemic, some precautions ended up being trivial—I will never forget wiping down my vegetables with Lysol. But the bulk effect of masking, washing hands, and distancing had a positive impact overall.

Conversely, to illustrate the impacts of inaction, let's look at how different approaches affected outcomes during the pandemic. While many countries implemented strict lockdowns and mask mandates, Sweden initially took a more relaxed approach, hoping to achieve herd immunity. This strategy prioritized keeping businesses open as usual and relied heavily on individual responsibility—in favor of normalcy. This controversial approach had severe consequences. By the end of 2020, Sweden's death rate was significantly higher than that of its Nordic neighbors. As of December 2020, Sweden reported 817 deaths per million inhabitants, compared to 107 in Finland and 81 in Norway. This stark contrast underscores how underestimating risks and failing to take preventative measures can lead to tragic outcomes.

This same reluctance to act is evident right now in our response to climate change. We desperately want to think that things will continue as they always have, with the massive hurricane or devastating fire being the random outlier, but all the scientific evidence suggests that these outcomes will only get more severe (STATUS QUO BIAS). Yet it can feel overwhelming to think of all the changes to our lifestyle and preventative measures that we need to implement for this future disaster, so we try our best to ignore it. However, this avoidance has far more serious consequences than arriving late to the airport: we are gambling with human lives, our homes, our economy, and our natural resources.

When faced with such decisions, it can be helpful to:

1. Consider how you might be underestimating the likelihood of a disaster or crisis.
2. Make a list of the best- and worst-case scenarios to put things in a more objective perspective.

For example, if you're thinking about climate change, consider the following: The best things that could happen are that you take action in reducing your carbon footprint, supporting renewable energy, advocating for sustainable practices, feeling good about making a positive impact, and inspiring others to do the same. The worst could be spending some extra time and money on lifestyle changes or facing resistance from those who don't agree with your actions. On the other hand, the best case if you don't take action could be avoiding short-term inconveniences and costs, while the worst case might be contributing to worsening climate change, more severe natural disasters, economic and societal instability, and a negative impact on future generations.

Thinking about potential outcomes in this way can help motivate us to take meaningful daily actions, even if they require some effort. Whether it's using less plastic, supporting local businesses, volunteering in our community, or advocating for causes we believe in, these small actions add up.

By anchoring your choices in your community, the environment, and future generations, you can make decisions that align with your values and contribute to a better world. Even the smallest steps in the right direction can lead to meaningful change when we take them together.

✳ BIASES TO EXPLORE

Illusion of control, pg 224:

We feel like we have more control over events than we do.

Optimism bias, pg 245:
We think we're less likely to experience a negative event than other people.

Normalcy bias, pg 242:
We tend to underestimate the likelihood and effect of rare disasters.

Status quo bias, pg 263:
We prefer that things stay the way they are, even if change would be for the better.

Good at Quitting

+ **QUESTIONS**

- Why am I so busy?
- Is there a more fulfilling job out there for me?
- How do I decide what to say no to?
- How do I make time for all of my interests and passions?
- How can I remove myself from situations that disempower me and take away my energy?

For much of my life, I have suspected that I'm a quitter. Someone who gives up when the going gets tough. As evidence, I have quit more than six jobs in my career, which is probably a few more than the average person. However, while quitting may seem like a negative trait at first glance, these repeated departures have shown me that it can also demonstrate a natural resilience in the face of uncertainty.

Quitting your job is rightly scary. Our jobs are often our main source of income, how we typically get health care, and where we build social networks. We often build lifelong relationships and amass expertise and institutional knowledge at our jobs.

Over time, our identities and self-worth can feel inherently connected to our titles and careers. Quitting can feel like losing all that. But just like anything else you practice frequently, quitting starts to become more approachable after a few test runs. You feel more comfortable because you can see it for what it really is: not just what you're losing but also what you're gaining.

Through my experiences with quitting, I've learned two valuable lessons:

1. There are often other, better opportunities available that you weren't aware of because you weren't looking.
2. These opportunities can create new and previously unimagined paths in your career.

As the dividends of these career moves have become evident, I've learned to reframe "being good at quitting" as "being opportunistic," which is a useful trait that helps me improve my situation.

There exists in all of us a strong tendency to keep doing something once we have invested time, money, or effort into it. This tendency applies to various aspects of life, whether it's a job, a relationship, a project, or any other decision. Because we have limited resources—only so much time in a week, money saved, and effort to give—we avoid wasting it. The feeling of abandoning an investment feels so bad, it's almost visceral. We try to avoid that feeling at all costs.

As a result, our decisions become emotionally swayed by past investments, even though the time has already been spent and there's no getting it back—and even when continuing is not the best choice. The more we invest in something, the harder it becomes to leave. The longer we spend on something, the harder it is to change course or start something new (SUNK COST FALLACY).

For example, imagine you've spent years climbing the corporate ladder in a company that no longer aligns with your values or career goals. The thought of leaving feels like throwing away years of hard work. But by focusing on what you've gained from the time you spent there—skills, experience, and relationships—rather than what you might lose, you can approach the decision more objectively.

In my own career, when making decisions about quitting I've learned to focus on what's being gained—taking advantage of opportunities as they arise, especially early on when I could afford to take risks—rather than focusing on the investments lost (FRAMING EFFECT). By focusing on the options being afforded instead of those being abandoned, I can offset the feeling of loss (LOSS AVERSION). Also, by remembering that my future self has emotional resilience and coping mechanisms (AFFECTIVE FORECASTING), I have been able to manage my expectations and reduce anxiety about the transition.

This mindset helps me realize that I can likely regain what I currently have, but I can't put myself in a better scenario if I'm not willing to let go. Certainly, leaving your job may not be the best move in every situation. However, remembering that we tend to overcorrect for safety and stability can allow us to approach seemingly risky choices with more courage.

By recognizing our natural tendencies and consciously shifting our perspective, we can make more balanced decisions that align with our long-term goals and aspirations.

While there is a lesson here about cultivating your risk tolerance when the stakes are low, I've found that the bigger takeaway for me was about changing my defaults (STATUS QUO BIAS).

In observing the unintentional cadence of my career, I've noticed that a two-year stint has worked well. A job of this length won't work for everyone, but for my industry and role, it gives me enough time to develop a fluency in the company, build working relationships, and understand if I can achieve quality work there. At the end of two years, I ask myself, "Would I hire this company to be my employer if I joined today?"

Nowadays, I approach new endeavors, like moving to a new city or starting a new project, with this point of view. By default, we tend to think about jobs, relationships, homes as being forever-ish—a fuzzy indefinite. But if we approach these opportunities with a check-in date in mind, we create a forcing function for ourselves. It becomes a built-in reason to ask ourselves the question "Why should I stay?" rather than "Why should I leave?"

The latter question causes us to hold on tightly to all the reasons why it's hard to leave. The former question acts as a gentle nudge to honestly check in with ourselves about all the reasons we originally chose to be in that situation.

Being good at quitting isn't just about impulsively jumping ship at the first sign of difficulty. It's about regularly reassessing your situation, being honest with yourself about whether it still serves your goals, and having the courage to make a change when necessary. By reframing quitting as a strategic tool rather than a last resort, you can ensure that you're making intentional choices that align with your goals and values, rather than simply holding on to the familiar.

✳ BIASES TO EXPLORE

Sunk cost fallacy, pg 266:
The more we invest in something, the harder it becomes to abandon it.

Framing effect:
We'll make different choices about information depending on whether it is presented to us in the context of a loss or a gain.

Loss aversion, pg 236:
If we have to choose between avoiding a loss or acquiring an equivalent gain, we'll value avoiding the loss higher.

Affective forecasting, pg 158:
When we try to predict how we'll feel about something in the future, we tend to overestimate both the intensity and duration of our emotional reactions.

Status quo bias, pg 263:
We prefer that things stay the way they are, even if change would be for the better.

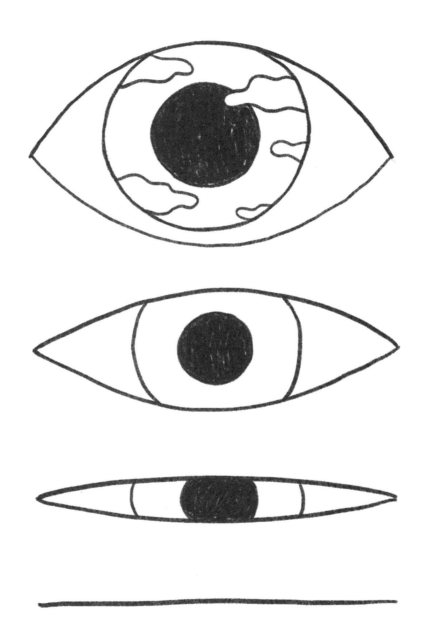

Newness

+ QUESTIONS

- How can I be more present?
- Am I getting enough rest?
- How can I regain my energy?
- How can I become inspired?
- How do I find joy?

Last fall, I spent a week in the golden hills of East Marin with a group of strangers in total silence. From afar, it must have looked like a summer camp filled with adults not having that much fun. We spent most of the day sitting with our eyes closed, then walking as slow as snails. We had taken a vow to refrain from talking to each other, including not making eye contact, and to give up all technology. This retreat was a type of meditation called vipassana, which focuses on equanimity, or mental calmness in formidable situations.

I've noticed that people seek out these types of retreats when they're at a crossroads—in need of a reset, or on either end of a big transition, searching for answers. I had wanted to take a retreat since I started meditating several years earlier, but hadn't found the right moment or perhaps lacked enough motivation to choose silence over an "easier" vacation.

Now I was at a moment when things had already slowed down. I had just moved back to California prematurely, to save money after being abruptly laid off from my job, and the quiet contrasted starkly with the energy of New York.

All of a sudden, my days were spent alone, struggling to write and feeling directionless. And with a midlife milestone birthday fast approaching, the time felt right. The silence was calling to me.

When you talk to people who have done vipassana, you'll hear a wide range of reactions. After a week in silence, some are ready to change everything, renounce material belongings, and devote their lives to the practice of mettā, or loving-kindness. Some feel despair, having seen with clear eyes the shallowness of their path. Others feel like they've been sent to solitary confinement and can't wait to speak out loud again. One friend told me she felt like she was going to die—something about the quiet had drawn out hallucinations of long-buried fears.

My experience was nowhere near as dramatic. What stood out at first were the many moments of boredom and just waiting for time to pass. Next came the physical pain from sitting for hours, cross-legged, while practicing meditation. After each half-hour sit, my body ached to stretch and move dynamically, to expel the stagnant energy that had built up. By the end of the second day, a low-key anxiety buzzed in my mind as I wondered whether I was doing it right—when would "the awakening" happen?

Beyond that, the tenor of the week was calm and slow. Following the monastic schedule started off challenging, then turned into a simple routine that I started to look forward to. Rise before the sun, sit to meditate, eat breakfast. That was followed by another sitting meditation, walking meditation, and lunch. The quietude turned mealtime into another moment to practice mindfulness: we were encouraged to chew slowly and, with each bite, think about the path that the food had taken to arrive to us, the hands it passed through, and the care that it took to bring it here.

Each person also had a small community work assignment every day, such as chopping vegetables, sweeping the floor, and taking out the trash. My job was cleaning the bathroom, which gave me the ick. I don't mind cleaning my own toilet, but cleaning a public toilet hits in a different way.

Remembering the guidance from our teachers—attempting to practice equanimity—I took a deep breath and focused in earnest on creating a clean and tidy place that everyone could enjoy using. The rhythm of the day was meditating, eating, walking, and sleeping. Written out like this it can sound banal—a life stripped of pleasure, excitement, and variety.

Despite my initial nervousness about giving up my worldly possessions, I was pleasantly surprised to find that I was not itching to check the things that I was typically glued to during the day: my phone, text messages, social media, the internet. Nor was I as dependent as I expected on my rituals of listening to podcasts, reading books, and talking with people. It was about halfway through the week when I had the realization that the magic of being there wasn't so much about what I was letting go of—technology, entertainment, socialization, alcohol, basically all modern forms of distraction—but in what that renunciation afforded: space to observe the mind.

Describing the concept of mental space is tricky because the interior landscape of the mind is unique to each person, much like the intricate patterns found in snowflakes. I envisioned my own mind as a zero-gravity chamber, a centrifuge where thoughts, ideas, and emotions float freely without any specific order.

When I find myself busy or overwhelmed, the velocity of this mental space intensifies, resembling a vortex. In this state, errands, aspirations, and ruminations take the form of thought-particles, swirling rapidly and colliding with one another in a chaotic dance.

It wasn't until the retreat that it felt like everything in the vortex had a chance to settle. As if I, who had been vigorously shaking my mind's snow globe, was finally able to put it down.

When the little white flakes finally came to a rest, I was able to observe the familiar surroundings without obstruction and with fresh eyes. I realized that the stimulating experiences I had been yearning for—the energy of a live jazz show, the thrill of a serendipitous park encounter, the buzzing potential of a Brooklyn summer night—were a type of novelty that captivated my attention (APPEAL TO NOVELTY) rather than teaching me to quietly attend to what was in front of me.

I've heard attention defined in two ways:[8] the first definition is that attention is what catalyzes awareness into action—a type of catalytic trigger.[9] The second definition is that attention (from the French *attendre*) means "to wait for." But to wait for what?

Philosopher Bernard Stiegler says that when we give something our attention, we are waiting for the ways in which we are connected to the object to become apparent.[10] And as we give that object or any living being more of our attention, we start to

8 Source: D. Graham Burnett, "Your Mind Is Being Fracked," *The Ezra Klein Show* (2024).
9 Source: Thomas H. Davenport and John C. Beck, *The Attention Economy: Understanding the New Currency of Business* (2001).
10 Source: Bernard Stiegler, *Taking Care of Youth and the Generations* (2008).

see those webs of connectedness mirrored in ourselves, showing us our own infinitude in the world.

For me, becoming settled in the familiarity of my surroundings taught me to give my attention in this subtler, gentler way that Stiegler described. Rather than expecting something to happen, I was able to shift my attention to a gesture of generosity, waiting in contentment, mirroring the nature, tending to myself.

This shift in how we understand attention can guide us to notice things we might have missed before, in a place we've been to a hundred times before, like the scent of crushed eucalyptus and pine beneath our feet or the sound of cicadas at dawn. When we're not being overstimulated, we can truly observe the landscape in front of us, finding solace without the need for constant novelty (CHANGE BLINDNESS). Once we understand that our attention is ours to give as patiently as we choose, in any moment, everything becomes new again, even in familiar surroundings.

✳ BIASES TO EXPLORE

Appeal to novelty, pg 167:
We think new things are more valuable than the same thing that's older, even if that's the only difference between them.

Change blindness, pg 185:
We can only pay attention to a couple of things at once, so we become blind to things that would otherwise grab our attention.

Full Circle

+ **QUESTION**

  • Should I become a parent?

On their first night away since becoming parents, my brother and sister-in-law tasked my mom and me with babysitting my nephews, Jack and Micah, aged three and two. My brother and sister-in-law had prepared them days in advance, telling them several times over how this sleepover would go, to which they gave an unfailingly enthusiastic response.

But when we arrived to pick them up from day care, Jack's face crumpled when he saw that we weren't with his parents. Tears welled up. We managed to patch things up, get everyone home, and make it through dinner and bath time with lots of chocolate milk and silliness. Throughout the evening, Jack kept looking toward the door, asking when Mama would be home, and we deferred his question to later and later, promising him that she would be home "as soon as you finish dinner" and "as soon as you brush your teeth."

The comforting veil of their nightly routine held up until bed-time, when following set instructions, we had to turn off the iPad. Removing the distraction of *Octonauts* was the last Jenga block sliding out of a shaky tower. It was as if a spell had been broken.

Chaos erupted. Over the next half hour, we endured full-volume wailing for Mommy and Daddy, a meltdown of epic pro-portions. He was inconsolable. No amount of hugs, kisses, or back rubs helped.

We comforted him the best we could as we waited for him to get sleepy. I remembered this younger, stubborn feeling of escalating a tantrum—the more you yelled, the more committed you became to the act of yelling. But within his wailing, I could also hear a deep fear that his parents would never come home. After all, this had never happened before, so who was to say they would?

At some point, while he was engulfed in his crying, I also became overwhelmed with sadness, hearing him say *Daddy* in the same way that I used to say my dad's name, and I was pulled back to the day that my dad did not come home. I was older than my nephew, twelve years old, but young enough to be confused by the weight of what his death meant.

Jack cried for hours until he fell asleep from exhaustion.

After my father's death, my mom moved on in the only way she knew how—she snapped into action. She didn't pause—she couldn't. The funeral preparations, the finances she didn't have access to, the mortgage for our beautiful and now too-large home, and raising two teenagers in a country away from her family.

Her grief was buried beneath a mountain of responsibilities. There was no time for tears, no space for vulnerability. In her eyes, our situation necessitated a bypassing of grief, jumping straight into surviving.

Feeling that connection with my nephew's fear surprised me, and I was able to glimpse the shadow of my younger self, which had been inaccessible for decades. I had learned from my mom how to be resilient, stay strong—a way to move on without question. But I hadn't learned how to accept my sadness, how to sit in my grief, how to feel my loss.

That night, I realized that we could not fully reassure Jacky that everything would always be okay, because sometimes dads do leave and never come back.

That night my heart broke a little for both of us.

When I asked my brother and sister-in-law how they decided to have kids, they both responded that it was inexplicable; they just always knew they wanted them. But if you, like me, are not one of those people, you might find yourself going through a more thorough decision-making process—starting by asking yourself *why* you want to become a parent, and what you would like to receive from parenthood, and how that might look in relationship to your partner, if you have one.

You can do your best to determine whether you would be able to support a child in the basic developmental ways they need. And if after all that consideration, you still find yourself wondering, you might then ask yourself what you are afraid of happening if you do or don't have children.

I can think of a whole bunch of fears of missing out: on the feeling of being pregnant, the awe-filled experience of child-birth, beautiful firsts—birthdays, steps, days of school. On not getting to experience the chapter of life that affords a new purpose and selflessness, a type of love unmatched.

And then there are other fears: about generational cycles, of a child becoming a parent, coming full circle. As I watched Jack cry for his parents, I couldn't help but wonder how my own loss had shaped my perspective on family and parenthood.

Reopening your history and confronting your past. Facing your fears of not being a capable and good-enough person who will rise to the occasion of parenthood. Or not having enough time and energy or tools to give the support that's needed. Wondering if you can give yourself to your child fully because of the ways that you were unsupported. Acknowledging a deep dread of failing your child in the same ways your parents failed you. Or even disappointing them in altogether new and different ways. There might also be a fear of bringing a child into the world with lacking systems of support, the sky-high costs of everything, school shootings, and existential dread about a warming planet.

There's this thing that happens, both as we grow up and throughout our lives. We will hear something so many times, from those around us or from society, that we start to believe it's true (ILLUSORY TRUTH EFFECT). It could be a criticism from a parent who didn't have the luxury of processing their own trauma. It could be the mainstream representation of what it looks like to be maternal or paternal. It could be this wisdom that we would know we were ready—when our biology told us so. It could be the platitudes that "there is no good time" and "you'll just figure it out."

We drown in other people's ideas of the joys and pitfalls of having children, struggling to discern what we want from what others want for us.[11]

I have a friend who decided to have two kids on her own. When I asked her how she made her decision, she emphasized that she

---

11 Social comparison theory is the idea that individuals determine their own social and personal worth based on how they stack up against others. The theory was developed in 1954 by psychologist Leon Festinger.

consciously chose to ignore societal expectations and perceptions of what it means to be a mother. She recognized that every child is unique, and therefore, general parenting advice and universal expectations often fail to capture the essence of being a parent— the interaction between two wholly unique individuals.

The journey to parenthood—or the decision to forgo it—is deeply personal, often messy, and always transformative. We are all part of this ongoing cycle of care, loss, and growth. The fears we face and the love we give contribute to our shared human experience. Perhaps the most profound aspect isn't the decision itself, but the self-discovery it prompts.

In the end, maybe the best you can do is try to dispel comparison to others. Let go of what you want your child to do for you, and instead ask yourself if you are prepared to provide them with what they need. Take this as an opportunity to give love fully, to heal in the act of repairing the things you wish had been different in your own life, and to enjoy the dual perspective of seeing with both a beginner's mind and the mind from the wisdom of your lifetime. You might just learn something about yourself along the way.

✳ BIAS TO EXPLORE

Illusory truth effect, pg 227:
When we see something repeated over and over again, we begin to believe that it's true.

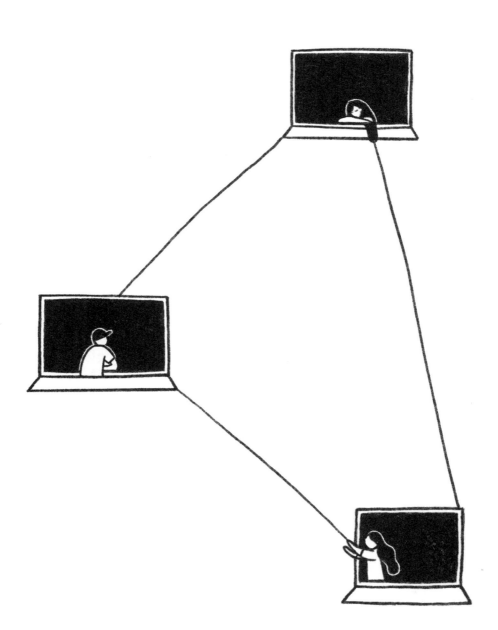

The Rickshaw

+ QUESTION

- How can I form deeper relationships?

I have a group of friends who I only know online, called the Rickshaw. I realize that spending hours talking to strangers on the internet carries a certain connotation, a stigma of being socially awkward or reclusive. But to me, here's what the Rickshaw provides:

Imagine having an intimate gathering with your most interesting friends who you don't get to see often or together, because of circumstances and proximity. Picture being able to listen actively to each of their stories, hear their intimate updates, and laugh at all their jokes. And then imagine being able to respond thoughtfully, after you'd had some time to digest the information. The beauty of an online community lies in these details—bringing together those spread apart, throttling the pacing of our interactions, the amplification of soft voices, and the ability for everyone to show up when they are ready.

This all started with my friend and mentor, Buster Benson, who I met online after he offered advice about a work disagreement that I was struggling to resolve. Conveniently, Buster was deep into writing his book *Why Are We Yelling? The Art of Productive Disagreement* and had started a small online community for early readers to share ideas and give feedback. The Rickshaw was named after jinrikisha (人力車), the human-drawn two-wheeled carts also referred to as pedicabs. Buster explained that he wanted to evoke the pace and intentionality of the human-drawn carts and their way of moving forward—the imagery in clear contrast to the rocket ship metaphor that most companies were using to describe their ideal trajectory.

For those unfamiliar with online forums, participation is optional and largely asynchronous. You can choose topics of interest and engage as you wish. Some members are very active, while others go silent for weeks. Contributing to the extent of your capacity is completely accepted and even encouraged. Collectively, communicating in this way creates a type of shared support network, without putting undue pressure on any single person.[12]

The description of the Rickshaw is: "A wide variety of people interested in a wide variety of topics. The culture evolving seems to be one of self-reflection, small projects, pattern languages, and appreciation and care for the complexity of life and each other." And our only connection to each other was that we were all unabashed fans of Buster. Some were avid users of 750 Words (his journaling platform), and others were fans of his cognitive bias work. I joined the group when I was exploring an early version of this book, in search of like-minded people who might want to collaborate. The Rickshaw's channels cover a wide range of topics, from #self-improvement and #book-club to #current-events and #storytime. There are also "sensitive" channels that formed organically, open to a subset of the group, where more personal inner thoughts tend to be shared.

But the internet is famously toxic, divisive, polarized—so perhaps it's more useful to consider why the Rickshaw is not that way. We were brought together by our shared interests in self-

---

12 Group cohesiveness is when we feel more unity, camaraderie, and mutual attraction among members of a group, which fosters a sense of belonging and commitment.

awareness, metacognition, feelings, and other hard-to-grasp lifelong topics of discussion. We are curious to learn more about our shared existence from each other, but with no expectations about how or when. This is a group of people who will listen without judgment and try their best to empathize with what I, or anyone else, am going through. They live in cities I've never been to around the world, have vastly different life experiences, backgrounds, identities, neurodiversity, and income diversity, culminating in points of view that I don't always get with my own friends, who are more like me than different. They may not always agree with me, but they will hear me and be honest in sharing how they feel. In different moments, they have all together been my biggest cheerleaders, my most transformative and honest group discussions, channeling decades of collective therapy, a journaling and fitness accountability club, and a treasure trove of exciting new ideas and thoughtful opinions.

My relationship with the Rickshaw evolved over time. At first, it was a place that I visited occasionally as a silent observer, similar in frequency to perusing a newsletter with a distanced curiosity. But with the inevitability of new jobs, moving cities, and breakups, I found myself unmoored from my usual routines and support networks. As my life circumstances changed, I realized how dependent my existing friendships were on shared contexts like neighborhoods, workplaces, or partners. I found—to my own surprise—that I was connecting more honestly and deeply with friends in the Rickshaw than some of my longtime friends.

In particular, I found myself gravitating toward the "sensitive" channels. Especially when I felt persistent anxiety, it seemed easier to share in the Feelings channel to no one in particular than to bother my best friend who lived thousands of miles away. If I wanted to vent about work, it felt less complain-y to do it in the Work Rants channel than to bring that negative energy to a night out with friends. And sometimes, in the middle of the night when I felt racked by doubt and indecision, it was a relief simply to be able to put the thoughts down, to have a place to write them out and leave them in an act of letting go.

This supportive dynamic became crucial during a challenging period in my life. Caught up in a complicated romantic relationship, I struggled to share honestly with my close friends. I found myself telling a filtered version of what was happening. On some level, I was embarrassed to say out loud that my boyfriend was emotionally abusive and that I felt trapped, at times even scared for my safety. Maybe I wanted to avoid an awkward conversation, or maybe I was dreading their reaction. Maybe I doubted my own interpretation of what was happening, an underlying current of shame causing me to retreat into denial.

It felt hard to shatter our mutual friends' view of my boyfriend and our relationship, made rosy by seeing only the good times on social media and when plans weren't canceled because of explosive arguments or emotional shutdowns. My best friends were intertwined in my life—they knew my boyfriend and had built up context (IN-GROUP BIAS). In the same way, they were limited in the advice and insight they could share. It feels paradoxical that our most intimate friendships are bound by politeness. Perhaps this stems from a respect for privacy, and a baseline assumption that we are all adults who have a handle on our own lives.[13] Or maybe it's just that our very best friends can't always share their unfiltered feelings *because of* our proximity and the fear of damaging that.

That was how I found myself, in my darkest, most hopeless moments, turning to the Rickshaw. I could send a message at any hour of the night, after an explosive argument, without worrying about bothering anyone. I felt supported knowing that there was always someone responding, listening, caring. No one person had any responsibility to respond, nor was I always looking for a response, but when someone did, it carried a special meaning. And unlike with a therapist, I got back stories of lived experiences and honest, real advice for how to do "the hard thing."

I desperately wanted to leave, but I couldn't find the courage or clarity to go. And it was only through the strong encouragement of these friends that I was able to take the daunting steps needed to get myself out of that situation.

Everything about the Rickshaw subverts what I learned about friends in my undergrad classes. Anthropologist Robin Dunbar theorizes that humans can maintain about 150 stable social relationships, with smaller inner circles of closer friends. According to Dunbar, it takes significant time and shared experiences—often hundreds of hours—to move from acquaintance to friend, and even more to become a best friend or intimate friend.

Professor William Rawlins has written about how friends

---

13 The bystander effect is a social psychology theory that suggests that we are less likely to help someone in distress when there are others around because we don't feel responsibility to take action.

serve three purposes: someone to talk to, someone to depend on, and someone to have fun with. The second category includes those who you count on in an emergency—no matter what happens, you can ask for help. This responsibility usually falls on your inner circles—your parents or siblings, romantic partner, and intimate friends. But what conditions must be met to depend on someone emotionally, physically, and mentally?

While these traditional models offer valuable insights, the Rickshaw demonstrates that we can challenge conventional wisdom by forming meaningful connection in whatever way that supports us. It has provided a special, tender, supportive form of connection. It has allowed me to form a whole new type of relationship safety net and create a chosen family that extends beyond geographical and social boundaries.

This isn't to say that I think you should ditch your closest real-life friends and rely solely on online communities. Rather, your very own Rickshaw could be found by joining a club or group that includes people outside your typical age range or interests, such as a meditation sangha, community volunteer organization, or a hobby-based group. Engaging with unexpected people in new settings can expose you to fresh perspectives, broaden the types of close relationships you have to friends who are completely unlike you, and explore new ways of interacting.

Of course, online communities like the Rickshaw aren't without their limitations. The lack of face-to-face interaction can sometimes lead to misunderstandings, and the asynchronous nature of communication can make it challenging to build the kind of rapport that comes from shared experiences in real time. However, for me, the benefits have far outweighed these potential drawbacks.

Take a look at your closest friendships and hold them in consideration. What do you love about your best friends? What else are you seeking from these connections? What social patterns or unspoken rules exist that are guiding your interactions? Can you be yourself, can you be honest, can you take off your social mask when speaking about contentious things? From these questions, you can start to find your own Rickshaw—your own inner-outer circle that isn't captured in Dunbar's circles—an unexpected type of friend group that can support you in unexpected ways.

✳ BIAS TO EXPLORE

In-group bias, pg 230:
We favor members of groups we belong to (the in-groups) over members of groups we don't (the out-groups).

Doomscrolling

+ **QUESTIONS**

- Why am I so tired?
- How do I deal with emotions like anger, fear, anxiety, and sadness?
- Why do I feel stressed?
- How can I have a healthy relationship with social media?

A few years ago, one of my best friends stopped going outside. She had been following news about the Asian hate crimes that had been escalating in New York City during the pandemic. Experiencing debilitating anxiety about being attacked, for the better part of a month she left home only when her boyfriend could accompany her.

During this time, multiple Asian-news-specific Instagram accounts popped up, sharing a constant stream of new reports about the attacks on Asian elders. Many of my Asian American friends found solace and kinship in this community; it was a safe space where they could share collective outrage and sadness. At the same time, it was disorienting to see these events amplified so loudly in my newsfeed while my non-Asian friends were seemingly unaware of the events going on in our cities.

My friend was certainly not the only one to respond in this way. The 2022 US Census found that Asian American households were twice as likely as white households to admit they didn't have enough food during the pandemic—not because they didn't have the money or ability to get groceries but because they were afraid to go outside. Within the community, the idea of being attacked felt so scary that it skewed our judgment (APPEAL TO PROBABILITY).

From 2020 to 2021, hate crimes against both Asian and Black communities saw significant increases. Asian hate crimes rose by 167 percent, from 279 to 746 per year. During the same period, anti-Black hate crimes numbered 2,871 to 3,277.[14] While the percentage increase in Asian hate crimes was larger, the raw numbers reveal a stark reality: according to this data, it was about four times more dangerous for a Black person to go outside than an Asian person.

While these hate crime statistics are alarming, it's important to consider them in the context of overall risk. Our perception of danger can be heavily influenced by media coverage and personal connections, sometimes overshadowing more common but less sensationalized threats. The surge in Asian hate crimes was likely due to scapegoating and anti-Asian rhetoric from irresponsible politicians, while systemic racism continued to fuel violence against Black individuals.

This comparison isn't meant to minimize the fear felt in the Asian community, but rather to illustrate how our perception of danger can be skewed by media focus and our own community connections.

14 Source: Uniform Crime Reporting Program, Hate Crime Statistics Federal Bureau of Investigation.

Given this complex landscape of real and perceived threats, it's crucial to understand how our minds process information, especially in times of crisis. We have a strong tendency to pay the most attention to information that feels bizarre or sensational to us (BIZARRENESS EFFECT)—in my friend's case, doomscrolling through posts about attacks on Asian people.

This effect is amplified by social media algorithms that prioritize engaging content, often leading to a feed filled with shocking or emotionally charged posts. The constant exposure to such content can significantly skew our perception of risk and reality.

It's natural to be drawn toward news about negative events because they have the potential to cause us much more harm. This anxiety is human—we have all felt this way in our worst moments. But the more dangerous result of this bias is that it can cause us to miss the warning signs of seemingly *boring*, but much more dangerous, threats.

If we look at the actual causes of death in the US in 2019, the top three were cardiovascular diseases at 957,455 deaths, cancers at 773,895 deaths, and respiratory diseases at 224,988 deaths. At the bottom of the list, conflict and terrorism accounted for 31 deaths.[15]

The mundane health threats are far more pervasive, but because they are slow dangers with slow solutions, they often don't grab our attention and effort.

Rumination can feel inevitable when you get sucked into a media black hole. Some people respond with vulnerable emotions—sadness, anxiety, and depression—while others respond with anger and an urge to take action. There were

---

15 Source: Global Burden of Disease (2019).

peaceful, organized rallies against anti-Asian hate crimes. I joined friends to launch a safety badge campaign and distributed these resources to community centers in our neighboring cities. Our campaign focused on creating visible symbols of allyship and support. We designed badges in multiple languages and made them open-source for bystander intervention groups and local support services. The initiative not only raised awareness but also helped many feel more connected and less alone in this moment.

Eventually, my friend found ways to take action and create more stability in her life. She unfollowed the multiple AAPI hate crime accounts that she had gotten accustomed to checking each morning and started seeing an Asian American therapist. She took time off work to focus on her mental health and signed up for new activities to get her heart pumping and her endorphins up.

Understanding how our minds work isn't a magical solution to rumination, depression, or anxiety; still, knowing how bias can affect your mental state can help you find something tangible and external to anchor to. By putting herself in a position to feel more control, my friend was able to start leaving the house again, with these new strategies also protecting her against longer-term health dangers. This experience taught us both valuable lessons about managing anxiety and cultivating a healthier relationship with social media. By recognizing our biases and actively seeking balance in our information consumption, we can better navigate the challenges of our digital age while supporting our inner well-being.

✳ BIASES TO EXPLORE

Appeal to probability, pg 170:
The mistaken assumption that if something is likely to happen, it's definitely going to happen.

Bizarreness effect, pg 179:
We tend to remember unusual, strange, or peculiar things instead of more mundane, everyday information.

Invariables

+ **QUESTIONS**

- Where is home?
- What does it mean to love?
- Who is my chosen family?
- Should I get married?

An energy percolates through my body as I ride my tiny 60cc motorbike along the steep mountainside of the Hải Vân Pass, a coastal road winding through the heart of Vietnam. The sensation is akin to diving into a pool—a full-body awakening. I scan the landscape, taking deep breaths, drinking in the view. My knees grip the tank for balance; my hands and feet rest on levers, ready to engage.

In physics, energy is defined as the ability to move matter, produce heat, and generate light. It cannot be created or destroyed, only converted. From the slope of the mountain to me. This energy is what drew me to riding and the open road. There's a palpable freedom in the caress of air against skin as the atmosphere parts to let me through. This, moving in concert with the well-oiled machine beneath me. Translating to "ocean cloud," the Hải Vân Pass embodies its name, a great sky dragon curling above the East Sea.

My riding partner and I were midway through our motorbike journey across the country, from Saigon and the Mekong Delta to the distant reaches of Hanoi and Ha Long Bay. We were a new couple who had started dating just a few months before, and I found my love of adventure well matched with his easy pick-up-and-go travel style. Within weeks of hatching the idea together, we were on a transpacific flight, each carrying a small backpack that would fit on the back of our motorcycles.

Before this trip, I was what they call a "fair-weather rider," cruising around San Francisco and along the coast for pleasure, never for commuting, always at a leisurely pace. My early-'60s Honda Super Hawk, lovingly nicknamed "Soupie," was an old café racer—high on style and low on speed, it was just right for me. I later learned it was the same model featured in Robert Pirsig's famous cross-country pilgrimage, *Zen and the Art of Motorcycle Maintenance*.

My fondness for two-wheeled machines began even earlier, when I learned to ride tiny mopeds. These pint-sized vehicles, no larger than a bicycle, took a kick to the pedals to bring their engines to life. When you accelerated, the sound could best be described as an obnoxious lawn mower. In the early aughts, they were the epitome of cool among city kids. My previous boyfriend was a moped builder who had shown me how to take care of these simple carbureted engines—the delicate balance of air, fuel, and oil that creates compression, the importance of cleaning the jets to allow proper airflow into the float, and how shifts in weather and atmosphere could necessitate a recalibration of the entire system.

This has been my favorite way to relate to another person, by learning and living their excitement together. More than lifelong partnerships, my relationships have been explorations into esoteric passions and new ways of being in the world. In my formative years, the music aficionado opened my ears to the deepest cuts of underground hip-hop, which planted the seed for me to cultivate a style of my own. The human-centered designer helped me discover my career path, while showing me what it means to navigate adulthood with purpose. With the woodworker, I learned to cherish objects and embrace a slower pace of life. And then there was the yogi, whose playful openness showed me the transformative power of vulnerability. Even though our paths ultimately diverged, each of these partners has been a teacher of their own making.

The idea of relationships as guides is echoed in Sheila Heti's book *How Should a Person Be?*, where she talks about the concept of *variables* and *invariables* in life. Variables are the flexible, interchangeable, and peripheral elements, such as friendships and community. These are parts of our lives that can be adapted or replaced as circumstances change. On the other hand, invariables are immovable; they require that we prioritize them above all else. Invariables often include family, long-term partners, and children.

In a sense, my past relationships are what Heti might call variables: flexible, interchangeable elements adapting to different phases of my life. And yet, each of these relatively short-lived connections has guided me toward peak moments in my life, like that cross-country motorcycle ride or giving my first design talk in front of a thousand people. Despite their transient nature, these *variable* relationships have been just as impactful as society's *invariables*, nurturing aspects of myself I never knew existed. They challenge the notion that only lifelong partnerships, like marriage, can be truly transformative. In fact, it may have been their very impermanence that allowed these connections to catalyze growth, proving that the depth of impact isn't determined by a relationship's expected longevity, but by its ability to shape us.

In our society, we often prioritize romantic love as the ultimate invariable, expecting it to fulfill all our needs and serve as the primary defining relationship in our lives (FUNCTIONAL FIXEDNESS). Esther Perel says that we ask our partners to give us what an entire village used to provide: belonging, identity, continuity, transcendence, mystery, comfort, edge, novelty, familiarity, predictability, surprise. But this narrow focus on a romantic partner can blind us to the transformative potential of other connections (FOCUSING ILLUSION). What if, instead, we allowed ourselves to find invariables in a wider array of connections? What if we recognized that different relationships could serve as stable, centering forces in our lives at different times?

I think of my friend Cha, who began as a colleague but quickly became so much more. As we've traveled across continents over the years, she has taught me invaluable lessons about compassion and how to truly see another person. In a similar vein, my sister-in-law, Aimee, has transformed our family dynamic in profound ways. Within our small family unit of three—my brother, mom, and myself—it was easy for one person to feel left out. Aimee's warmth has brought a new sense of connection, changing the way in which we interact with each other. Her generous expressions of love and affirmation have helped us all become better at openly showing our appreciation for one another. These nonromantic relationships have been equally as impactful as the romantic ones, if not more so, in their slow, steadily maturing, and gently nonexpectant nature. They have expanded my understanding of what an "invariable" connection can be.

Realizing this helped me appreciate each relationship and its own ability to be transformative, whether easy or challenging, whether it lasts for decades or months. This shift in framing helps me approach new connections with openness and curiosity, rather than rigid expectation.

In the end, perhaps the most transformative realization is that our invariables—the relationships that ground us and guide us—can take many forms. A mentor, a chosen family member, a lifelong friend, a trusted community presence, a peripheral tie, a consequential stranger—each of these connections can be driving, steady, and regenerative energies in your life. While a life partner can certainly be a centering force, so too can any other connection of any duration or nature. By following where the energy leads us, releasing the grip of preconceived notions, expected outcomes, and the need for definitive endings, we can open up to the kaleidoscope of ways we have yet to become ourselves in this world.

✳ BIASES TO EXPLORE

Functional fixedness, pg 209:
We tend to use an object only for its intended purpose.

Focusing illusion, pg 206:
We tend to place too much focus on one aspect of a decision, while neglecting other crucial factors. This narrow focus can distort our thinking and lead to inaccurate conclusions.

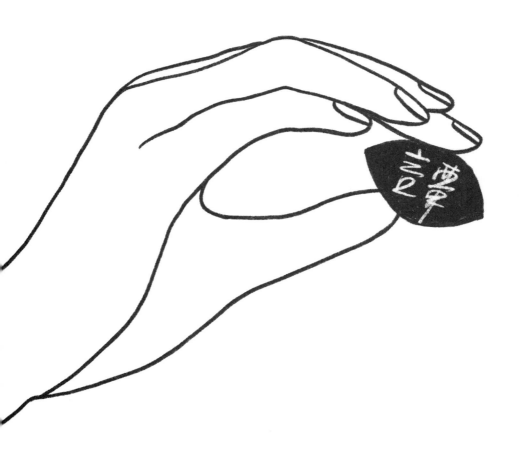

Futureless

+ **QUESTION**

• How can I spend less and live within my means?

Over the years, growing up around many Chinese immigrant families like my own, I've noticed that the same unspoken rules apply: the guests take off their shoes as a sign of respect, and the hosts offer food as a gesture of love. It was comforting to discover recognizable details around their homes: an old Danish cookie tin used to store odds and ends, dishwashers used as drying racks—never for washing—and wrapping paper and bows carefully saved for next year's Christmas. These familiar sights and practices were like discovering clues of a subtler culture in common.

These shared practices weren't just about cultural identity; they reflected a deeper philosophy about money and resources. We were a family of middle-class immigrants from Taiwan. Both of my parents had come to the US to get their graduate degrees and had good jobs. Our diligent saving wasn't about the money—it was about being *nonwasteful*. It was a reminder to be thoughtful about spending.

Instead of buying disposables, we splurged on longer-term investments: family camping trips, tennis coaches, dance lessons. We were taught to save up for what we wanted and then buy it once we had enough money. Credit cards were for accruing good credit rather than fulfilling future wishes (MENTAL

ACCOUNTING). But these rituals did not preclude generosity; our parents, aunties, and uncles were always trying to sneak away to pay the dinner bill before the rest of the party noticed. It was like a universal Chinese dinner game that they all played with each other. These practices made me wonder: Where did these cultural norms come from?

One possible explanation for these behaviors may lie in the structure of the Chinese language itself. The theory of linguistic relativity suggests that language shapes our mental construct of the world. Chinese is what linguists call a *futureless* language—there are no conjugations for the past, present, and the future. In English, you say that yesterday *you ate*, today *you eat*, and tomorrow *you will eat* something delicious. In Chinese, you simply say that *you eat*, whether it's yesterday, today, or tomorrow. In this way, the Chinese language doesn't imply that time is chopped up into distinct parts; rather, it flows on a continuum where the past and future are closer in proximity to the present.

This linguistic fluidity may subtly guide the spending habits of native Chinese speakers, encouraging financial decisions that prioritize long-term benefits, as if the future is a neighboring home rather than a distant land. While these theories are debated among linguists, the idea of language tacitly influencing our behavior remains a fascinating concept (BELIEF PERSEVERANCE). Whether it's our language that has influenced these behaviors, or perhaps the broader cultural mentality that influenced the language, this way of spending feels ingrained in me.

This idea of inherited wisdom reminds me of a concept from one of my favorite books. In "The Bookmaking Habits of Select Species," sci-fi novelist Ken Liu describes a fantastical creature called the Quatzoli, whose minds are made of stone. Over their lifetimes, their stone minds form intricate mazes of millions of tiny paths carrying the water of their thoughts—this creates their consciousness. Each of their stone minds is like a book, holding a record of all the wisdom accumulated throughout their life. When a Quatzoli has a child, they give a sliver of their stone mind as the seed for their child's mind to form around. Physically encoded in this piece of stone are their most durable values, to be passed on for generations to come.

In a similar way, the seeds of saving have been encoded within me, as ancestral gifts from my parents and their parents. And while my unique expression of these tenets has been shaped by my environment, I've maintained familiar rituals as a reminder of nonwastefulness: making homemade granola, saving and regrowing green onions in a cup of water. These habits help me avoid lifestyle creep and treadmill-style hedonism. Lifestyle creep occurs when spending increases in tandem with rising income, while treadmill-style hedonism refers to the cycle of constantly needing more purchases to maintain satisfaction.

Instead of constantly chasing new purchases, I've learned to find joy in quality and intention. I splurge on objects that bring me joy in my daily routine: aromatics, skincare, and objects that feel special when I inhale, feel, and touch them each morning. I spend on purchases that help me feel balanced and healthy, like a yoga membership, fresh local produce, or nice trail-running shoes. When you find quality objects that attend to your values, you can get *more* value out of them as time goes on.

Even if you didn't grow up speaking a futureless language, you can still adjust your mindset to think more long term. Identify the purchases that have the most meaning to you by looking at what has brought you value over the years, and find intentional ways to upgrade those objects (TIME DISCOUNTING). And find your version of a nonwasteful ritual, to serve as a daily reminder to be thrifty and take care when you spend. These behaviors will help remind you that your future is closer to this present moment, and that all moments are worth saving for.

✳ BIASES TO EXPLORE

Mental accounting, pg 239:
We tend to think about money differently based on how we mentally categorize, value, and prioritize it.

Belief perseverance:
We tend to avoid revising our past or current beliefs, even when presented with new evidence that contradicts them. Meaning, even after we've officially decided to change our mind about something, some parts of the old belief will linger.

Time discounting:
We value things in the present more than things in the future. A type of **affective forecasting, pg 158**.

Pentel 0.5mm Lead

+ **QUESTIONS**

- How do I deal with emotions like anger, fear, anxiety, and sadness?
- Why do I feel sad?

Pens and pencils have always been my number-one favorite office supply. I feel like they have the ability to transform your entire persona. A gliding rollerball, an inky fountain pen, or a soft felt tip each offers a completely different experience on a sheet of paper. The thickness and shape of the pencil, whether rounded or polygonal, undoubtedly influences your grip. The softness and thickness of the lead, ranging from 2B to 2H, and the width of 0.5mm or 0.7mm for those who prefer less precision, reminds me of the reed in a woodwind instrument. Just as the reed affects the sound of the instrument, your choice of writing implement changes the timbre of your writing.

The office goods store we were in that day feels so familiar, but I can't recall the name. It was a ritual to stock up before the school year started, like going to Blockbuster on Friday nights to rent a VHS or the Wherehouse on weekends to find new-release CDs. I can imagine its circular floor plan, with rows of shelves in concentric arcs leading to the register. I relished in the precise organization of all the tiny things living tidily in their designated drawers.

One of the only memories I have of my dad is from one day in that store. Somehow, already a budding kleptomaniac, I had the idea to steal ten sticks of Pentel 0.5mm lead. Perhaps the smallest and cheapest item in the entire store, I covertly transferred the contents of one pack of lead refill into another, the slim diamond tube holding my secret booty. When my dad and I went to check out, I held my breath and kept my gaze downcast.

The clerk noticed the tube and asked my dad if he knew how that had happened, all the while looking suspiciously at me. This part I remember most vividly. Without missing a beat, my dad came to my defense. Standing there mute, I felt the simultaneous swelling of pride and cowering shame, holding both truths in my body.

When my dad died, it was sudden, without any of the typical warning signs of heart failure. He was healthy, active, and young, at that moment playing basketball with friends on a Sunday morning. With his death, it seemed as if all my memories of him also died. The day he was supposed to come home, I hid inside the cabinets in our kitchen island, sitting in the dark alongside cereal and rice, hearing discussion in hushed voices.

In the months and years after, we learned as a family how to *chī kǔ* (吃苦). The literal translation of this phrase is to "eat bitterness." The bitter taste has a double meaning in Chinese—the taste of bad fortune. To chī kǔ meant to persevere through hardship without complaint or suffering, to swallow what had been given. We did not cry, we did not mope, and we did not waste time feeling sadness. We maintained a steady state of mind, rather than letting ourselves feel emotions that lead us off the rails (STATUS QUO BIAS). Imagine a deep well, nearly overflowing with immense amounts of water from recent rainfall. Then imagine forcing a lid on the well, shutting it all down. That's how you chī kǔ.

Emotion is a word that is often used interchangeably with *feeling*. Only recently have I come to understand the difference between the two. Feelings are sensations in our body: a racing heart, a sinking pit in the stomach, a flutter in our chest. Emotions are our brains making sense of the sensation, telling a story about the feeling. Imagine your cerebral cortex acting as a weatherperson labeling the feeling of sun radiating heat as a "beautifully sunny day," or labeling the water dripping from the sky as a "dreary rainy day." These forecasts are your brain's best guesses about how the day will go based on how things went in the past. And these are emotional labels that are written early on in life. They act as reference points for how we should interpret feelings in the future (ANCHORING EFFECT).

By resisting sadness, I blocked the feeling out of my body, similar to the act of shuttering the windows on a cloudy day, anticipating the rain coming in. When my dad died, my brain created a model of the world that labeled sadness as useless. As I grew up, my brain confirmed this hypothesis, selectively remembering instances when this perseverance allowed me to succeed or move forward in an effective way, ignoring the times when I was restricted or unable to express vulnerability (CONFIRMATION BIAS). It prepared my body for the weather so I wouldn't have to brace for the rain. In doing so, I also shut out fresh air, the cool breeze, and the wetness of the rain.

Remembering is defined as the ability to bring to mind or think of again. While on a meditation retreat, my teacher reframed it as *re-membering*, to reconnect with the members or parts that you've cut off. To feel the sensations in your body that you have blocked off. To become whole again.

It wasn't until decades later that the memory of my dad in the office goods store came flooding back to me, along with all the other details about that moment in my life. It was as if by reconnecting with my feelings, I had unlocked a part of my mind that had been hidden away, waiting to be rediscovered.

Once I allowed myself to welcome the feeling of rain, to stop thinking of it as an interruption to my life and let it envelop me, I began to recover the memories I'd lost. Like a frog, hopping in the rain—not thinking of the millions of small drops of water as terrible weather, but instead as the immense, unstoppable rush of life.

✳ BIASES TO EXPLORE

Status quo bias, pg 263:
We prefer that things stay the way they are, even if change would be for the better.

Anchoring effect, pg 164:
We rely too heavily on the first piece of information we receive when making decisions.

Confirmation bias, pg 191:
We interpret information in a way that confirms our existing beliefs.

✳ BIASES ✳

Exploring your biases through an open-ended format reminiscent of tarot or Enneagram can encourage you to engage in deeper introspection, curiosity, and experimentation.

Each bias is presented as a spectrum of behaviors, inviting you to consider multiple interpretations rather than a single takeaway. By recognizing both the strengths and weaknesses of each bias, you can start to identify when it's beneficial and when it's limiting your perspective.

This balanced approach to understanding biases can help you lean into what your mental models are already doing well while becoming more aware of their potential pitfalls. Through a series of reflective prompts, you'll develop a more nuanced understanding of your biases, creating a space for increasing your self-awareness and embracing new perspectives.

Allow yourself to question your assumptions and consider alternative viewpoints. By engaging with each concept in a curious and open-minded manner, you'll gain valuable insights into how biases shape your thoughts, decisions, and actions.

✳ **Stories**

Yancey's Mustache, pg 63
Memory-Foam Pillow, pg 91
Good at Quitting, pg 107

⊙ **Keywords**

emotions,
feelings, coping,
anticipation,
future

Affective Forecasting

When we try to predict how we'll feel about something in the future, we tend to overestimate both the intensity and duration of our emotional reactions.

Affective forecasting is our tendency to underestimate our ability to emotionally cope with negative events in the future. In other words, when we try to predict how we will feel about something bad happening in the future, we underestimate our natural resilience and our brain's natural ability to adapt and move forward. We assume that the negative event will impact us more strongly and for much longer than it actually does. Recognizing this in the moment can help us make more realistic predictions and clear-headed choices about the future.

Light

Promoting realistic emotional expectations, reducing anticipatory anxiety, fostering emotional resilience, reducing unnecessary worry, acting with wisdom toward future self, nourishing resilience, boosting confidence when facing challenges, promoting mindfulness

 Shadow

Experiencing excessive worry and chronic anxiety, wasting mental energy, avoiding potentially rewarding experiences, shying away from change, having a pessimistic outlook, undervaluing personal resilience, having unrealistic emotional predictions

Prompts

1. How is your current situation being influenced by how you think you will feel in the future?

2. For any negative outcomes that you are worrying about, what neutral or positive outcomes are also likely to occur?

3. Can you recall times when you were surprised to find that humor, relaxation, or rational thinking naturally made the moment smoother?

4. Can an experience help you gain understanding and wisdom, even if it's uncomfortable in the moment?

5. What are some examples from your past when you have shown resilience in the face of adversity?

6. How might recognizing the temporary nature of most emotions influence your outlook?

Life

When you are feeling worried or anxious, you may sometimes hear a little voice in your head attempting to predict how you will feel in response to a particular situation. To help counter this tendency, try writing a letter to your future self using a website like FutureMe.org, where you can compose an email and schedule it to be sent to yourself at a future date. In this letter, try to write in the way you would to a close friend who you care about deeply and include the following:

1. Details about the current situation you are worried about and your fears surrounding it.

2. Reminders of past experiences where you faced similar challenges and how you successfully coped with them.

3. Words of encouragement, reminding your future self of your strengths, resilience, and ability to handle difficult situations.

4. A realistic outlook on the upcoming event, acknowledging that while it may be challenging, you have the skills and support to navigate it.

Schedule the letter to be sent to yourself shortly before the event you are concerned about. When the time comes, read the letter and allow the perspective and encouragement from your past self to bolster your confidence.

By reflecting on your past experiences and reminding yourself how you've successfully coped with similar challenges, you can trust in your ability to handle the upcoming event. Writing a letter to your future self serves as a tangible reminder of your resilience and can help you approach the situation with a more balanced view.

✳ **Stories**

Hsu Ken's Dad, pg 79
Trees, pg 85

⊙ **Keywords**

aversion,
discomfort,
unknown, risk,
fear, luck,
uncertainty,
predictability,
probability

Ambiguity Effect

We choose options that are more certain, even if those options are likely to be worse.

The **ambiguity effect** is our tendency to prefer clear options over ambiguous ones, even when the latter could result in something better. We are uncomfortable with unknown options because they are difficult to evaluate. Instead, we prefer clear, precise, known probabilities because they are easier to assess. Minimizing unpredictability can show up when deciding to stick with our favorite restaurant rather than trying a new, potentially better one, or taking our same, familiar route to work, even though a different route may save time.

Light

Exercising caution for major decisions, promoting prudence, making calculated decisions, taking known risks, favoring stability and conservatism, maintaining consistency

 # Shadow

Missing opportunities, avoiding the new, being reluctant to welcome change, reinforcing the status quo, feeling stagnant, narrowing experiences, limiting personal growth, overlooking potential benefits

Prompts

1. When was the last time you tried something completely new, with no research or agenda or predictability to the experience?

2. Imagine making a choice by closing your eyes and pulling the answer out of a hat. What emotions does this bring up?

3. Are there any decisions that you've considered but ultimately did not end up making, such as a career change, a relationship, or a new hobby?

4. Do you tend to take risks or play it safe? What do you think drives this behavior?

5. When a path or decision feels daunting, what are some ways you can increase your understanding of it? Is there research you can do, people you can talk to, or a low-stakes way to try it out?

Work

When we are feeling creatively stagnant, it might be because we have rigid expectations of how the creative process should look and feel. Release your expectations of what you think will result from it. Progress thrives in the realm of questions, concepts, and embracing the unknown.

Lean into the messiness, and explore the new sensations that come up when you do. Wander through unfamiliar neighborhoods, sit in a coffee shop without your phone, and leave a note on a community bulletin board. Strike up a conversation with a stranger at a bookstore. Go to karaoke and sing as loudly as you can. Spark the conceptual collisions that can help you break out of your creative rigidity.

Purpose

Reflect on the moments in your life that felt "lucky"—meeting someone who ended up becoming a close friend or longtime collaborator, stumbling upon an ideal job opportunity, or discovering your favorite restaurant. Consider the idea that these moments occurred, in part, because of your openness.

To invite more happenstance into your life, trust in serendipity and spontaneity, and loosen your fixation on a well-planned path. Actively seek out new experiences and step out of your comfort zone, as this can increase the likelihood of encountering unexpected opportunities. Luck tends to reveal itself in the unexpected and the peripheries. As David Whyte puts it, "What you can plan is too small for you to live."

✳ **Story**

Pentel 0.5mm Lead, pg 151

⊙ **Keywords**

anchor, initial value, first impressions, starting, arbitrary, overreliance, priming

Anchoring Effect

We rely too heavily on the first piece of information we receive when making decisions.

The **anchoring effect** is our tendency to rely too heavily on the first piece of information we receive when making decisions or judgments, known as the "anchor." Even arbitrary or irrelevant anchors disproportionately influence people's assessments and conclusions by causing them to stay closer to the starting anchor than they would otherwise. For example, our first impressions of people can become social anchors that influence how we think of their subsequent generosity, trustworthiness, or kindness.

Light

Motivating better outcomes, anchoring to personal bests, being strategic in negotiations, allowing new evidence to sufficiently adjust judgments, assessing information objectively

 Shadow

Forming arbitrary impressions that influence opinions, failing to adjust from first impressions, underestimating warning signs based on previous experiences, judging people based on first impressions, overlooking alternative perspectives

Prompts

1. Have you noticed your first impression of something strongly guiding your later assessments, even when you receive new, contradictory information?

2. Reflect on a recent big decision. Without analyzing it, think about the very first piece of information you received. How might it have consciously or subconsciously guided your choice?

3. Reflect on a situation where you had to make a judgment call without having all the facts. What information did you rely on to fill in the gaps, and how might this have influenced your conclusion?

4. Think about a time when you were learning about a new concept or skill. What preconceptions did you bring to the learning process, and how did these initial reference points help or hinder your understanding?

Life

We often overlook how big of an impact our physical states, such as hunger and tiredness, can have on our emotions and, consequently, our decisions. Physical states can create initial impressions that serve as anchors, shaping our perceptions and preferences.

For example, a college student attending an early-morning math lecture while hungry and tired might form a negative impression of the class, which could lead them to drop the course. However, if the same student had attended the lecture later in the day, well rested and on a full stomach, their experience could have been more positive, creating a different experiential anchor that could have changed their decision to stay in the class. It's easy to overlook these physical factors because we have become accustomed to ignoring them. By tuning in to our physical sensations and being mindful of how they affect our thoughts and feelings, we can make more informed and balanced choices, especially when the decision is irreversible.

Relationships

When you first met your partner, you bonded over your shared adventurousness, taking international trips and exploring new activities every weekend. Years into marriage and parenthood, life looks more stable and routine. You find yourself yearning for those thrilling early days, but your current reality, finances, and obligations don't allow for those types of extravagant trips anymore. It's easy to anchor to memories of daring exploration together, which can cause you to feel boredom and resentment, creating a feeling of having "become dull." Instead, notice how your reality has shifted and focus on the present joy of having a compassionate partner to grow with.

✳ **Story**

Newness, pg 113

⊙ **Keywords**

newness,
innovation,
trends, change,
value, status quo,
stability

Appeal to Novelty

We think new things are more valuable than the same thing that's older, even if that's the only difference between them.

The **appeal to novelty** is our tendency to think that new things or ideas are better simply because they are novel. This excitement and interest in novelty itself is what creates a feeling that new things are automatically an improvement over the old. When we do this, we tend to overlook whether the actual quality, functionality, or merits of the new thing are better than the old. In the same way, this also means that we tend to undervalue the status quo or what already exists.

Light

Driving innovation and progress, adapting to evolving challenges, seeking out new experiences, discovering new approaches to old problems, embracing technological advancements, challenging outdated paradigms

 # Shadow

Overlooking value and quality, discarding things prematurely, conforming to trends, lacking stability and continuity, ignoring historical learnings, wasting resources on unnecessary upgrades

Prompts

1. Do you find yourself more drawn to familiarity or novelty, whether in relationships, work, technology, or lifestyle?

2. Do you find yourself excited or reluctant to try something new? Are you content to stick with what is already working?

3. What is your relationship to trends and what's currently popular? How does this influence your buying behavior for clothing, accessories, and the like? How does the relationship between quality and quantity affect your buying choices?

4. Is it challenging to stick with routines or the same habits over long periods? Or do you enjoy stability and consistency?

Life

Health and lifestyle trends are important to evaluate carefully, in particular because social media has the ability to amplify fads that may not be backed and validated by science. Whether it's a new diet, type of exercise, supplement, or sleep aid, make sure to take time to evaluate both its merits and effectiveness compared to your current routine.

Let's say, for example, you have been maintaining a balanced diet with a range of fruits, vegetables, whole grains, and lean proteins. This routine generally helps you feel healthy and energetic. When a new superfood is promoted as a miracle with superior health benefits, you are eager to add it to your diet. Before doing this, take time to understand how it will complement your nutrition, what foods you are already eating that provide the same benefits, and what downsides this supposed superfood might have that are specific to you.

Relationships

In long-term relationships, it can be enticing to introduce something new and exciting to reignite the spark that you might have felt more strongly at the start. Pause to consider whether your desire for change is driven by an unmet need for something specific or if you are being drawn to the thrill of the novel. If the former, engage in an open and honest conversation about what each person needs. If you both decide to try something new, consider the existing dynamics, what is already working well, and how that might affect your shared values and goals.

Story
Doomscrolling, pg 133

⊙ **Keywords**
probability,
likelihood,
improbable,
chances,
ignorance,
considerations

Appeal to Probability

The mistaken assumption that if something is likely to happen, it's definitely going to happen.

The **appeal to probability** is our tendency to think that if something is likely to happen, it's definitely going to happen. In the same way, if we think something is unlikely, we'll treat it as impossible. You may have heard of Murphy's Law, which says that "anything that can go wrong will go wrong." However, just because something is possible doesn't mean it's probable, and just because something is probable doesn't mean it's certain.

Light

Making informed decisions in uncertain or ambiguous situations, planning for contingencies, being thorough and considering all outcomes

 ## Shadow

Engaging in superstitious rituals, making risky health or financial choices, neglecting safety precautions, being careless in evaluating available information, ignoring historical patterns and change over time, making decisions based on fear

Prompts

1. If there was a 30 percent chance of rain, would you bring an umbrella? Why or why not?

2. Do you tend to act as if something is guaranteed just because it's likely?

3. What unlikely outcomes might you be overlooking because they seem rare?

4. Are you being more cautious in making a decision because there's a chance of something negative happening? Are you being overly optimistic when there's a chance of something positive happening?

5. Are you relying on a limited set of personal experiences or anecdotes? How can you broaden your perspective before you come to a decision?

Health

Exercise can be a paradoxical thing because sometimes it doesn't feel enjoyable, especially if you haven't been exercising regularly. To make matters trickier, you often don't notice the health benefits immediately. While those who exercise regularly may boast that they feel energized or get a runner's high, that might not be your experience. So it's easy, then, to decide to not incorporate exercise into your routine, thinking that you've been perfectly healthy without it. But an absence of health problems now doesn't mean that regular movement isn't necessary. It just means that you have been fortunate so far or that the effects of not exercising aren't showing up yet. Remember that health outcomes are complex and influenced by many factors, and make a decision based on a more holistic understanding of your health.

Work

When you've been with the same company for several years, you may start to feel a deep connection with the organization. You may have formed close relationships with your colleagues, feel comfortable with the workload, and enjoy the lifestyle that comes with a steady income. While you've been seeing layoffs in your industry, you might not feel too worried because your company seems stable. You think about all the time and effort you've dedicated there and feel a sense of security with your job, making you less motivated to explore other opportunities.

But the reality of the situation is that organizational dynamics can change quickly, economic conditions can shift, and industries evolve. Balance your hard-earned sense of stability by staying up to date with your knowledge, researching other potential companies, and keeping in touch with those in your industry.

✳ **Stories**

Charlie the Dog, pg 43
Buoyancy, pg 51

⊙ **Keywords**

focus,
concentration,
perception,
selectivity, tunnel
vision, openness

Attentional Bias

If we think about something, we'll notice it more in our day-to-day.

Attentional bias is our tendency to home in on certain details, thoughts, or information while ignoring other potentially relevant information. So, if we start thinking about something, we'll notice it more in our day-to-day. The ability to focus intently allows us to concentrate and filter out distractions, but it can also create tunnel vision, causing us to ignore alternative possibilities or viewpoints. Learning to zoom out and see the big picture can help us stay open-minded.

Light

Being able to focus deeply, perceiving signals in noise, concentrating on priorities, avoiding irrelevant distractions, letting in the information that feels most important

 ## Shadow

Thinking rigidly, prioritizing details that confirm beliefs, fixating on what's in our focus, missing unconventional solutions, willfully ignoring information that challenges our comfortable narratives

Prompts

1. Can you identify any mental ruts or rigid thought patterns you have?

2. What inputs (conversations with people, reading books, listening to podcasts) have you sought out to add flexibility to your thinking?

3. How certain do you feel about your narrative or point of view? How do you feel when others share opinions that are different from your own?

4. How might your emotional state be influencing what you pay attention to?

5. How could you practice noticing details that you typically overlook?

Relationships

Pet peeves are a type of attentional bias that can show up in our relationships, whether it be with family, roommates, or partners we live with. We can become so fixated on one small detail, for example, a messy kitchen, that we overlook other chores that our housemates have done that are out of our line of sight: paying bills, laundry, and grocery shopping. This selective focus on the pet peeve—dishes in the sink—can lead us to feel like our housemates aren't pulling their weight.

Being aware of our ability to shift our attention can also help us appreciate all the things that our partners do for us. Rather than nitpicking about what's left undone, make a list of things that you are grateful for. Instead of obsessing over the mess, ask yourself: How has your family, roommate, or partner done something to show care and support?

Purpose

When you reflect on your life, your attention may gravitate to times of productivity, success, and external validation, while overlooking seasons of exploration, rest, and stillness that nurtured inner growth. This attention toward tangible accomplishments can lead you to value career and external growth while minimizing internal aspects like creativity, presence, and community that provide fewer tangible outcomes.

Widening your perspective balances appreciation for both external contributions and inward cultivations that give your life purpose. Broadening your attentional lens can provide a fuller picture of how you're actually living your values in this lifelong journey.

✳ **Story**

Trees, pg 85

⊙ **Keywords**

memory,
importance,
information,
mental, recall,
thoughtful,
consideration

Availability Bias

We tend to favor the options that come to mind easily. Things that don't, for whatever reason, are at a severe disadvantage.

The **availability bias** is our tendency to assume that what comes easily to mind must be more common or true. Therefore, when making decisions, we consider only the options that are easily recalled. Things that we can't remember quickly, for whatever reason, are at a severe disadvantage.

Understanding this bias helps us pause and take time to consider other options that may be less memorable. Because we have a natural tendency to favor what pops into our mind first, we can think of these as more important. Keeping this in mind can act as a gentle nudge to pay attention and give due weight to things that we may have more difficulty recalling.

Light

Making decisions quickly in familiar situations, possessing heightened awareness of potential risks, processing information efficiently, prioritizing relevant information, recognizing patterns rapidly

 ## Shadow

Jumping to conclusions without full context, ignoring a thoughtful or longer process, being impatient, not thinking things through before acting, neglecting less memorable but important information

Prompts

1. What's a recent decision that you made quickly? Are there any perspectives or options you might have overlooked?

2. What might present itself as a new, interesting, or valid opportunity in any aspect of your life if you allowed yourself more time to investigate it?

3. Consider a habit you've been trying to change. What strategies immediately come to mind for breaking this habit? Are there any less obvious approaches you might be neglecting?

4. When was the last time you intentionally delayed a decision (the last time you "slept on it")? Could you apply this approach to other aspects of your life where you tend to make quick and confident decisions?

Life

Imagine yourself at your ninetieth birthday party. As you reflect on your life, notice which memories and achievements come to mind first. These easily recalled moments might be shaping your perception of what a fulfilling life looks like. Now, challenge yourself to think beyond these immediate recollections. What quieter, less dramatic experiences might you be overlooking? Perhaps there were small, daily acts of kindness or perseverance that, while less memorable, were equally important in shaping your life's journey.

Now consider your daily routine. Which activities dominate your thoughts and energy? Are these truly aligned with your long-term goals, or simply the most recent or pressing concerns? Take a moment to consider less obvious but potentially more impactful ways to spend your time. By consciously expanding your focus beyond what's readily available in your mind, you might discover a more balanced path toward your future self.

Purpose

Before making important decisions, create space for stillness. Notice which options come to mind first, likely influenced by recent experiences or frequent advice. While valuable, these immediate thoughts may not represent all possibilities.

Challenge yourself to look beyond initial ideas. What might you be overlooking simply because they're less prominent? Consider seeking diverse information sources or perspectives. By counteracting availability bias, you can broaden your understanding of yourself and the world. Reflect on your guiding values and beliefs. Are these truly your own, or shaped by easily accessible societal norms? Questioning the origin of your thoughts can help you develop your own sense of purpose.

Bizarreness Effect

We tend to remember unusual, strange, or peculiar things instead of more mundane, everyday information.

The **bizarreness effect** is our tendency to better retain and recall odd or unexpected information compared to ordinary, everyday details. Bizarre things things stand out because they catch our attention and require more effort for us to understand. While this might seem harmless and interesting, it can be a distraction that takes our attention away from much more dangerous things that seem familiar or boring.

Light

Noticing patterns to find meaning in deviations from normal, having enhanced emotion and recall, thinking outside the box, experiencing heightened engagement

 ## Shadow

Prioritizing novelty over truth, having reduced attention span for the ordinary, overlooking the mundane but important, experiencing fatigue from overstimulation, recalling distorted or inaccurate memories, being distracted from critical information

Prompts

1. When making a life transition, can you consider the ordinary and routine—for example, your meals, the community around you, your physical surroundings, the quality of your sleep and rest—as well as the bigger, more unusual aspects of your decision?

2. Have you noticed yourself adding significance to a weird coincidence based on how much it is sticking out in your memory?

3. How might the novelty of potential options be disproportionately influencing your preferences over more ordinary but reliable options?

4. When you're considering a new friend or romantic partner, how much weight do you put on more unusual personality quirks or obscure interests rather than how aligned your values are? What is the impact of prioritizing relationships in this way?

Relationships

Imagine you and your friend go on a hiking trip together but accidentally take a wrong turn and find yourselves lost in the woods. You encounter a series of unexpected sights, like a hidden waterfall, plants you've never seen before, and a mysterious hobbit-like home hidden in the moss.

Though the experience is initially stressful, you both find yourselves laughing at the absurdity of the situation and marveling at the strangeness of it all. This unique shared experience, filled with bizarre twists and turns, creates a distinctive memory that stands out in your minds and becomes a bonding moment in your friendship that you both look back on fondly. Embracing the unusual and unexpected elements of your shared experiences can create lasting memories that strengthen and add depth to your friendship.

Purpose

The pivotal points in life are easy to recall—a life-changing moment that happened after following your gut, or a close call with disaster that felt like a lucky string of events. These peak experiences can cause ordinary days to fade into the background.

When looking forward or backward, keep in mind the bigger truth: that these big life moments happen in concert with your daily routines. A lifelong habit of awareness helped avoid that accident. Little acts of hard work created the foundation for that big life opportunity. Find gratitude for the normalcy in your life. Consider the feeling of being content or even bored as a sign that things are going well. Remember, we can find meaning in dramatic, memorable moments—and also in the underlying patterns of our everyday routines.

+ **Questions**

How can I be more
productive and achieve
my goals?

How can I feel my
creative energy again?

⊙ **Keywords**

height, space,
environment,
perception,
creativity,
problem-solving

Cathedral Effect

**Working in spaces with high ceilings has a positive
effect on creativity, and vice versa.**

The **cathedral effect** is the relationship between ceiling height
(real or perceived) and our approach to problem-solving. Working in spaces with high ceilings has a positive effect on creativity and abstract thinking. (The other, lesser-known half of this
effect is that low ceilings promote concrete and detail-oriented
thinking.) This can show up as a feeling of being free and lib-
erated rather than confined or restrained. The cathedral effect
can influence your preferences, and in turn how you evaluate
and make decisions. More generally, this tendency is a good reminder that our "containers"—our perceived spaces—have a
constant and easily overlooked impact on us.

Light

Harnessing heightened power of creativity, having the freedom to imagine, thinking outside the box, stimulating ideas and innovation, fostering expansiveness, encouraging big-picture thinking, enhancing spatial awareness

 Shadow

Feeling confined, disregarding space and environment, having a narrow focus, being close-minded, missing the bigger picture, having a concrete outlook, harnessing limited creative potential

Prompts

1. How might your physical spaces be influencing your perception of your mental space?

2. How willing are you to explore or to take an abstract view of the world? How frequently do you find yourself in a focused, detail-oriented mode of thinking?

3. What upcoming decisions might benefit from unorthodox ideas and fresh perspectives? Which might require more analytical or logical thinking?

4. How might you modify your environment to suit different cognitive needs?

5. When have you noticed a shift in your thinking based on your surroundings?

Life

If you are feeling creatively stagnant, begin by brainstorming ideas for opening up your space, whether at work or at home. Even if you don't live in a home with high ceilings, the perception of height matters more than the actual height. Techniques that emphasize the vertical nature of your room and draw the eye upward can also create the same effect:

- Draw attention to the height of your room with the furnishings. Include tall mirrors, standing lamps, and plants that have a vertical expansiveness, like a palm or fig tree.

- Paint your walls and ceilings a lighter color. The lighter the color, the taller the walls will seem. Matching the color of the walls and ceiling creates a continuous vertical plane for your eye to follow.

Work

When doing creative work, do your best to pay attention to your environment when in different phases of a project. High ceilings can stimulate more abstract and innovative thinking, which can often be helpful at the start of a project. As you refine and narrow in on a solution, consider finding cozier or closed spaces to get to that final decision.

Purpose

Construal level theory suggests that people can adopt two mindsets: abstract and concrete. High construal or abstract thinking will help you evaluate a forest, and low construal thinking will help you evaluate a single tree. When making a decision related to purpose and existence, consider whether you want to employ more boldness, risk-taking, and broad thinking.

✳ **Story**
Newness, pg 113

⊙ **Keywords**
limited attention, unnoticed changes, invisible, gaps, blindness, undetected, imperceptions

Change Blindness

We can only pay attention to a couple of things at once, so we become blind to things that would otherwise grab our attention.

Change blindness is a phenomenon where we fail to notice big, obvious, visual shifts that are right in front of us. This happens because your brain can handle only a couple of tasks at a time, so it focuses on paying attention to and watching those. Change blindness reveals limitations in our perception—namely that it can be influenced by our experience and our environment, rather than being a continuous, detailed representation of the visual world. An example of this is an experiment in which you watch a video of a basketball game and are asked to count how many times the players in white pass the ball, during which you likely miss the person in a gorilla costume walking through the group.

Light

Experiencing attention efficiency, filtering nonessential details, focusing on meaningful information, finding consistency in experience, reducing sensory overload, promoting selective attention

 ## Shadow

Experiencing misunderstandings, having tunnel vision, perceiving inaccurately, experiencing unreliable recall, overlooking relevant information, missing environmental cues, having decreased situational awareness

Prompts

1. How would you describe your level of awareness when going about your daily routine? Are there any subtle changes or details that you might have overlooked that could be impacting your happiness?

2. When you are faced with multiple tasks at once, how do you prioritize your attention? What gets overlooked?

3. How much attention are you paying to the evolving dynamics of your relationships? Are there any cues or changes you might be overlooking?

4. Take a moment to do a body scan. Are there any underlying patterns or changes in your physical or emotional state that you might be missing in the busyness of your day-to-day?

Life

If you've ever asked yourself, "Do I drink too much coffee?" you may be tapping into your intuition about your daily consumption habits. To answer this question, you can experiment by periodically taking a break. If you find that you're feeling calmer and less anxious and are sleeping better, you may want to reset how much coffee you drink each day, or switch to matcha or decaffeinated coffee.

When you take a pause, you bring awareness of change blindness over time, and it can help you be more intentional about your caffeine consumption. This practice can be applied to alcohol, chocolate, and other things that we might build a sensory tolerance to over time.

Purpose

At the beginning of each new year, many of us set aspirational resolutions and goals, envisioning the positive changes we want to make in our lives. Throughout the year, however, our habits, priorities, and activities evolve gradually through our day-to-day choices, and these incremental changes often go unnoticed as they accumulate over time. End-of-year reflections can often reveal how much we've drifted from our original goals, highlighting where adjustments are needed.

Setting more realistic, incremental goals for the coming year can help us stay connected to the process of change. Regularly checking in on how our habits and activities are slowly shifting allows us to evolve more intentionally. Consciously noticing small changes as they happen in real time enables us to counteract change blindness and progress toward our aspirations with greater awareness.

✴ **Story**

Trim Grass, pg 73

⊙ **Keywords**

coincidences,
meaningfulness,
lucky streaks,
superstitions,
magical
thinking, luck,
pattern-seeking,
randomness

Clustering Illusion

We tend to see clusters and streaks in data that aren't really there.

The **clustering illusion** is our tendency to perceive random and chance groupings or clusters of events as meaningful or purposeful. This happens because we want to find patterns and make them more meaningful than they are, so we connect the dots even when there is no real connection. This can result in superstitions or a feeling that coincidences have significance. In particular, the clustering illusion is common in sports and gambling, when people feel like they are experiencing a "lucky streak."

Light

Uncovering connections, finding meaning in chaos, sparking curiosity, having improved confidence and morale, building momentum, generating new ideas, motivating further exploration, fostering a sense of purpose

 ## Shadow

Developing false explanations, drawing inaccurate conclusions, perpetuating harmful superstitions, engaging in misjudgment of risk, having overconfidence in predicting future events, wasting resources on meaningless investigation, overestimating significance of chance clusters

Prompts

1. Think about the last time you felt lucky. What went through your mind about why this was happening? Did you feel like what was happening was random, or was there a predictable pattern?

2. Do you have any personal superstitions, rituals, or customs that you believe will positively or negatively impact you? Explore what emotions might be at the root of these beliefs.

3. When you experience misfortune—especially moments when many bad things have happened at once—what conclusions have you come to?

4. Reflect on the role that pattern recognition plays in your life. When has it served you well, and when might it have led you astray? What can you learn from these experiences?

Life

It's natural to seek meaning and patterns in events around us. The stories we construct based on perceived clusters can powerfully shape our understanding and experiences. Some clustering sparks creative bursts and novel connections—beautiful innovation often happens this way. The patterns we recognize can profoundly impact our mindset and emotions, providing a sense of control and purpose amid uncertainty. However, it's crucial to recognize that not all patterns are meaningful; clustering can lead to overinterpreting coincidences or drawing conclusions from limited evidence. By balancing pattern recognition with careful evaluation, we can harness clustering's power while minimizing its drawbacks.

Purpose

Our brains are wired to find order in chaos, leading us to see familiar images, like Jesus on toast or Mother Teresa in a cinnamon bun, even when they aren't really there—a phenomenon known as *pareidolia*. This tendency leads us to spot shapes like bunnies and dogs in fluffy clouds or perceive a man in the moon. By embracing this natural inclination, we can harness it to create personal narratives that give our lives a greater sense of purpose and direction. We can craft stories that help us feel fulfilled and guided toward our goals, even amid life's uncertainties. Consciously shaping narratives based on perceived patterns can be a powerful tool for personal growth and emotional resilience.

Confirmation Bias

We interpret information in a way that confirms our existing beliefs.

The **confirmation bias** is our tendency to search for, interpret, favor, and recall information in a way that confirms or supports what we already believe to be true. We tend to seek out information that supports our beliefs, ignoring that which contradicts our views, and interpreting or remembering ambiguous things in a way that supports our views. This filtering happens unconsciously and can be very challenging to recognize in yourself. It can lead to overconfidence in our personal beliefs, stereotyping, and echo chambers.

Light

Taking shortcuts for navigating complexity, efficiently processing information, maintaining consistency and stability, building confidence in decision-making, reinforcing existing knowledge, focusing on familiar patterns

 # Shadow

Being close-minded, resisting change, hindering intellectual growth, seeking inaccurate information that aligns with preconceptions, fueling polarization and division, creating echo chambers of thought, promoting narrow and rigid thinking, perpetuating blind spots, ignoring contradictory evidence

Prompts

1. Have you ever had a gut feeling about something that you later found out was wrong? What influenced your initial intuition?

2. What sources of information do you regularly engage with across news, social media, and friends? How do you react when you come across an article that challenges your existing beliefs?

3. Reflect on a disagreement or misunderstanding you had with someone close to you. Were you truly listening to their perspective, or could you have been focused on defending your own position?

4. Can you think of a time when your assumptions or preconceived beliefs misled you in some way? How might more openness have created an opportunity to explore other perspectives?

Life

Confirmation bias can sneakily infiltrate your daily life, often unnoticed. When scrolling through social media, you might gravitate toward posts aligning with your existing beliefs, feeling validated while dismissing challenging information. This subtle act of engaging with confirming content gradually reinforces your views, making it harder to consider alternative perspectives or engage in open-minded discussions. Take the discomfort of contradiction as a cue to engage more deeply, and with curiosity.

Relationships

Have you labeled a friend as flaky due to frequent last-minute cancellations? When they cancel for a family emergency, you might immediately see it as another example of unreliability. You may focus on and remember the times they've not shown up, while overlooking instances of dependability. When discussing this friend, you might share complaints about their absences, seeking validation for your annoyance.

Instead of reinforcing this belief, actively consider alternative explanations for their behavior and recall times they've been reliable. Engage in open, honest communication with your friend about their situation, expressing care while listening to their perspective.

✳ **Story**
Mapo Tofu, pg 57

⊙ **Keywords**
finance, money,
budgeting,
spending, time,
value

Denomination Effect

We're less likely to spend large denominations than small ones, even if the amount is the same.

The **denomination effect** is our tendency to treat different denominations of our limited resources—such as money, time, or effort—in distinct ways.

For example, we often spend small amounts carelessly, and these minor expenses can add up to large sums we wouldn't normally spend. Conversely, we're usually more hesitant to use large amounts, like committing to long time periods or spending big lump sums. This aversion can make big goals seem harder to reach than they really are. Understanding this effect helps us be more mindful of how we use our resources for things that matter to us.

Light

Being thrifty, having prudence with spending and debt, saving for the future, being willing to spend larger amounts of money on goals that have long-term rewards, investing in valuable activities, taking on new opportunities with the long term in mind

 Shadow

Being ignorant of daily spending, overlooking recurring charges, being frugal rather than looking for larger ways to save money or time, focusing on short-term things that feel satisfying but aren't as meaningful

Prompts

1. How do you decide what to spend money on? How do you decide how to spend your time?

2. How thrifty are you? How generous are you? Are you the same with your time and money?

3. What was the last big goal that you felt was out of reach, due to a lack of money or time? Was there a way that you could have found the resources for that goal?

4. What was your last big purchase? What was the effect of this purchase on your life?

5. How might you reallocate how you spend your time and money within the bigger context of your life goals, rather than what's in front of you?

Life

Being thoughtful with how you use smaller amounts of money and time can have an outsized impact, as the value builds up over time. For a spending gut-check, export year-end summaries from your bank and credit accounts to see what you spent total on streaming, eating out, or going out for drinks. As one friend put it, "I just learned that it only takes $27.30 a day to spend an extra $10,000 a year and suddenly my fun drinks and sweet treats aren't so fun."

Similarly, for time, pay attention to your "time confetti," those little pieces of time floating around in your day. Because these moments are small and dispersed, it's hard to recognize that they add up to bigger chunks of time, so we often let that time confetti float away by scrolling endlessly on our phones. Using these smaller moments to connect with loved ones, practice mindfulness, or express gratitude can improve your time affluence.

Work

Think about a goal that feels out of reach. This could be finding a new job or taking time off to work on personal projects. Start by writing out all the details of this goal in a wish list or on a visual mood board. Then review your calendar to see whether you're actually using your free time toward these tasks. (If you don't actively use a calendar, try experimenting with this for the next month.)

Now compare how important this goal is to you with how much time you're actually spending on it each week or month. If you find there's a gap between your goal's importance and the time you're dedicating to it, use your calendar review to identify areas where you could potentially free up some time. Look for activities you might be able to reduce or eliminate to make more room for pursuing your goal.

※ **Stories**

Yancey's Mustache, pg 63
Hanger Math, pg 67

⊙ **Keywords**

self-perception,
confidence,
humility,
beginner's
mind, learning,
expertise

Dunning-Kruger Effect

When those of us who lack skill or knowledge tend to overestimate our abilities, and those of us with more knowledge or skill tend to underestimate them.

The **Dunning-Kruger effect**, sometimes referred to as **illusory superiority**, is our tendency to overestimate our own qualities and abilities. This can cause us to think we are more competent, intelligent, or skilled compared to others. It is also called the "above average effect," because most people rate themselves as above average for positive characteristics. Conversely, it can also lead those with high abilities to underestimate their own competence or expertise because they have a greater awareness and understanding of their field. By being aware of this tendency, we can help ourselves cultivate a more realistic and objective self-view.

Light

Cultivating humility, being open to learning, building confidence in uncertain situations, embracing the unknown, approaching challenges with the confidence to grow, having heightened self-awareness, seeking out constructive feedback

 ## Shadow

Having overconfidence and hubris, feeling superior to others, making bold claims without expertise, dismissing the perspective of others, resisting learning and self-improvement, believing that one's opinion is the only correct one, dismissing criticism as invalid

Prompts

1. How confident do you feel in your work and relationships? Are there specific areas where your confidence is higher or lower?

2. Are there people you can trust for their honest opinions and feedback? When you have received challenging feedback, how have you responded?

3. How comfortable are you with saying "I don't know" and asking for help in uncertain situations?

4. How might you balance humility and confidence in your abilities?

5. Have you felt defensive when someone questioned your expertise? What does this reveal about your relationship with uncertainty and learning?

Life

In early 2021, a frenzy of investments in GameStop captured the attention of many atypical investors, including younger and less experienced people. These investors were drawn in by on-line discussions that led them to feel knowledgeable about the intricacies of day-trading stocks, leading to an overconfidence in their ability. Despite lacking a strong understanding of market dynamics and the unpredictable nature of these financial trades, they were driven to make risky investments based on their *perceived* expertise. To avoid falling into this trap, it's crucial to rely on thorough research and a deep understanding of the fundamentals of an investment, rather than getting swept up in hype from social media or other sources. Seek direct advice from a financial expert to get guidance and help prevent impulsive decisions based on overconfidence.

Purpose

Approaching life with Zen Buddhism's concept of a "beginner's mind" means always staying open, curious, and ready to learn without fixed ideas, no matter how much experience or expertise you possess—much like how a beginner or a child approaches new things. This mindset allows you to embrace the unknown, question your assumptions, and discover novel insights that might otherwise be overlooked. By staying humble, exploring different paths without expectations, and being receptive to guidance from unexpected sources, you can maintain a flexible attitude, fostering curiosity and continuous learning in the quest for your life's purpose.

✳ **Stories**

Buoyancy, pg 51
Hsu Ken's Dad, pg 79

⊙ **Keywords**

investment,
self-assembly,
co-creation,
overvaluation,
emotional
attachment, pride
of craftsmanship

Effort Justification

When we work for something, we end up valuing it more. Some people also refer to this as the IKEA effect.

Effort justification is our tendency to attribute greater value to an outcome that we had to put effort toward. The more effort, pain, or energy we invest in doing something, the more we value it. This happens because we don't want the effort we've already invested to be wasted. So to avoid feeling regretful or foolish for putting in so much effort, we place more meaning and value on it, after the fact. The IKEA effect, named after the furniture retailer known for selling self-assembly products, demonstrates how the act of building something increases our sense of ownership, accomplishment, and emotional attachment to the product.

Light

Increasing perceived value and meaning, having greater appreciation, feeling a sense of accomplishment, steadfastly following through, valuing process over results, enjoying hard work

 ## Shadow

Overlooking flaws, having the inability to quit or change course, feeling stuck to past work, pushing through burnout, overlooking easier paths, overrationalizing hard work

Prompts

1. Was there ever a time when you poured your heart into something that didn't turn out as expected?

2. What goal or project are you currently pursuing? Are you valuing any parts of the process more because they feel hard-won?

3. Is there a relationship or commitment that feels effortful or depleting? Could you be overvaluing it because of how much you've invested in it?

4. Can you think of a time you took the easy route and got a great result?

5. What is the value of effort versus outcome?

Relationships

Imagine you have a friend or family member who has gone through a challenging period in their life. You've invested many hours listening, offering advice, and providing emotional support. However, as time passes, you realize that the relationship has become imbalanced, and this pattern is recurring. Your friend continues to rely heavily on you but rarely reciprocates the support or takes steps to improve their situation. Take a moment to acknowledge your own feelings of being drained and unappreciated. Consider how you might communicate your emotions and needs to your friend in a caring but clear way. Pause to reevaluate the relationship based on its current dynamics, rather than feeling obligated to persist because of all the support you have given. It's okay to set boundaries and advocate for your own well-being, even in long-standing relationships.

Existential

Imagine pouring years into a passion project, only to face disappointment when it doesn't succeed as hoped. It's natural to search for meaning in this perceived failure, thinking, "All that effort must have been for something." This reaction often stems from the discomfort of accepting that significant investments sometimes don't pay off as expected. Your effort and dedication were valuable experiences, regardless of the outcome. Appreciate the growth and learning that came from the process, rather than justifying the time spent based solely on the result.

✳ **Story**
Hanger Math, pg 67

⊙ **Keywords**
attachment,
ownership,
identity, loss
aversion, loyalty,
possession,
hoarding

Endowment Effect

We value things that we own more than what we don't, regardless of the real value of the items.

The **endowment effect** is our tendency to value an object more highly when it is part of our "endowment" or ownership. For example, you might be willing to pay twenty dollars to acquire an item, but if you already own the same object, you might demand thirty dollars to give it up. This may be caused by loss aversion, and the pain of losing something being greater than the pleasure of gaining it.

Light

Feeling a sense of pride and ownership, cherishing memories, appreciating sentimental items, being loyal to commitments, investing in homes and communities, preserving traditions and heritage, fostering a sense of belonging

 ## Shadow

Giving in to materialism and clutter, being reluctant to leave, having the inability to let go of ego or identity, defending possessions or ideas at all costs, clinging to sinking investments, engaging in territorial conflicts, feeling entitlement, hoarding resources, accumulating unnecessary possessions

Prompts

1. What emotions arise when you consider letting go of an object you've owned for a long time but no longer use or enjoy?

2. Consider an item you treasure deeply for its sentimental value. How does your emotional attachment affect your perception of its worth?

3. Have you ever kept something useless because getting rid of it felt like wasting money?

4. Think about an identity you've had for a while. How can you see if this label is still serving you?

5. Have you experienced a conflict over a shared resource or territory? How did you handle it?

Life

Being aware of our tendency to overvalue items we own can help improve purchasing decisions by enabling us to make a more objective assessment of an item's value before buying. If you're considering a fancy espresso machine, try renting or borrowing a similar one first to experience "ownership" without commitment. During this trial, take notes on how often you actually make espresso and whether you're enjoying it as much as you anticipated. Lastly, make sure to look up return policies in advance to create an easy out in case you're not satisfied with your purchase.

Purpose

The people we know, the things we do, and the groups we belong to shape who we are—they all become part of our "endowment." The more time and energy we invest in these areas, the more they become a core part of our identity. This can lead us to overvalue these aspects of ourselves and resist changes that might actually help us grow. We might cling to old ideas about who we are, even when these ideas limit us.

To avoid getting stuck, try to be aware of how strongly you're attached to different parts of your identity. Practice being more flexible in how you see yourself. Remember, who we are and how we present ourselves to the world can change over time. By embracing this idea, we open ourselves up to new experiences and personal growth, rather than being held back by outdated self-perceptions.

✳ **Story**

Invariables, pg 139

⊙ **Keywords**

overemphasis,
tunnel vision,
selective
attention,
shortsighted,
oversimplified

Focusing Illusion

We tend to place too much focus on one aspect of a decision, while neglecting other crucial factors. This narrow focus can distort our thinking and lead to inaccurate conclusions.

The **focusing illusion** is our tendency to place too much importance on one aspect of an event, decision, or situation, while neglecting other crucial factors. When we focus intently on a single factor or detail, our thinking can be distorted, causing us to overestimate its significance and impact. This bias can lead to inaccurate judgments, predictions, and decisions, as we fail to consider the bigger picture and the complex interplay of multiple variables.

Light

Paying attention to detail, thoroughly considering specific factors, analyzing deeply, identifying key influences, recognizing personal values

 Shadow

Oversimplifying complex situations, neglecting broader context, making inaccurate predictions, engaging in flawed decision-making, overlooking important variables

Prompts

1. Recall a time when you were extremely focused on or worried about one thing. In retrospect, how much did it truly impact your overall well-being and happiness?

2. Have you made a prediction or judgment heavily influenced by a single piece of information? Looking back, what other factors should you have considered?

3. How often do you take the time to step back and consider the larger context and the interconnectedness of all the factors that may be at play?

4. Think about the small, everyday things that bring you joy or peace. How often do you notice and appreciate these compared to focusing on larger worries or desires?

Life

Imagine that you're working on a challenging project and feel stuck. While taking a break, you see a friend's post about a new productivity technique that seems like the perfect solution to your problem. You become fixated on this technique, believing it will be the key to help you overcome your roadblock. However, by focusing too heavily on this single solution, you may be overlooking other important factors that contribute to your productivity, such as the project's complexity, your skills, and the need for collaboration. If the technique doesn't end up helping as much as you expected, you may feel disappointed or discouraged due to your overemphasis on its potential impact. In the future, start by finding the real cause of your challenge, gather a few solutions from family members or mentors or experts in the field, experiment with different strategies, and reflect on your approach by checking in with yourself to see what's working.

Relationships

If you're single and want to be in a romantic relationship, you might fixate on the idea that finding a partner will unlock your happiness and fulfillment. You may spend hours swiping on dating apps, imagining your ideal match, and dreaming of the joy a new relationship might bring. However, by focusing too intensely on this one aspect of your life, you risk neglecting the importance of cultivating happiness in other areas. Remember that while romantic partnerships can contribute to your overall happiness, they're not the only source of it. To create balance and fulfillment, nurture strong friendships, pursue hobbies and interests, and prioritize personal growth through self-discovery. By broadening your focus and embracing the many facets of life, you'll build a strong foundation for happiness, regardless of your relationship status.

Story

Invariables, pg 139

 Keywords

fixed, rigid,
narrow, stuck,
constrained,
inflexible,
adaptability

Functional Fixedness

We tend to use an object only for its intended purpose.

Functional fixedness is our tendency to only see objects for their usual function. When we encounter an object, our mind fixates on its traditional use, making it challenging to recognize alternative ways it could be used, especially in problem-solving situations. This mental block hinders creativity and outside-the-box thinking. By becoming aware of this bias, we can train ourselves to view resources more flexibly. For example, if we need a paperweight but only have a hammer, we won't always think to use the hammer as a paperweight.

Light

Capitalizing on reliable tools, using tried-and-true methods, leveraging existing knowledge, maintaining consistency, upholding tradition

 # Shadow

Stifling creativity, missing innovative solutions, using limited problem-solving, resisting change, overlooking hidden potential

Prompts

1. When faced with a challenge, do you find yourself defaulting to familiar approaches? How willing are you to try unconventional methods?

2. Think of a time you used an object in a new or different way. What inspired you to get creative with it?

3. Are there any areas of your life where you feel stuck in a rut? How might challenging your assumptions about your resources help you break free?

4. Think of any skills or exceptional talents that you possess. How might you repurpose or adapt these abilities to solve problems or create value in other areas of your life?

Relationships

Functional fixedness can create challenges in relationships when partners have inflexible ideas about each other's roles in household tasks. For example, if you've always been the one to cook meals, you might feel frustrated or unappreciated when your partner tries to start cooking their own meals in the kitchen. Instead of viewing this as an intrusion in your domain, consider how their interest in cooking could be an opportunity for connection and shared responsibility. By releasing the belief that you alone are the "chef" in the relationship, you open the door to new experiences and a more equitable distribution of labor. Embracing adaptability in your roles can foster a more collaborative and fulfilling partnership, one where both individuals feel valued and encouraged to explore their interests and abilities.

Purpose

When juggling a busy schedule, it's easy to feel like each activity is a separate and time-consuming commitment. You might feel like you don't have enough hours in the day to exercise, socialize with friends, read for pleasure, and spend quality time with family.

To overcome this mindset, challenge yourself to reexamine the ways in which you can combine and blend different aspects of your life. For example, invite friends to join you for a weekly walk or bike ride, combining exercise and socializing. Similarly, starting a family book club can blend quality time and intellectual pursuit, fostering new types of conversations between family members. By letting go of the notion that each activity has its own time and function, you can open yourself up to a world of possibilities for combining and integrating the things that matter most.

✳ **Story**

Charlie the Dog, pg 43

⊙ **Keywords**

context, situation, circumstance, compassion, self-awareness

Fundamental Attribution Error

We tend to attribute other people's behavior to their personality rather than to external circumstances.

The **fundamental attribution error** is our tendency to explain other people's behavior through their personality traits, while explaining our own behavior through our circumstances. For example, if someone else is late to a meeting, we might think they're disorganized or lazy. But if we're late, we're more likely to blame external factors like heavy traffic. We give ourselves the benefit of the doubt, considering the context of our actions, but often fail to extend the same courtesy to others. Recognizing this bias can help us be more empathetic toward others and more accountable for our own actions.

Light

Promoting personal accountability, having awareness of how circumstance affects behavior, enabling empathetic social interaction, fostering growth through recognition of individual agency

 ## Shadow

Making flawed assumptions about others, fixating on personality rather than context, overlooking the context and situational details, not giving others the same benefit of the doubt as oneself

Prompts

1. Recall a time when a friend's behavior annoyed you. What was your initial explanation for their actions? How might considering their circumstances change your interpretation?

2. Think of a stressful situation that caused you to act unusually. Did others consider the context you were in?

3. In making decisions, how do you balance immediate circumstances against your typical behavior? Can you remember a choice where situation outweighed personality?

4. When making important decisions, how much do your circumstances (like time pressure or available resources) tend to affect your choices?

5. Think of someone whose actions puzzle you. What unseen factors might be influencing their behavior?

Life

When someone frustrates us, it's tempting to get angry and judge their character. Instead, remember that we're all "broken machines," as George Saunders puts it. Each person has their own struggles and experiences shaping their behavior.

Next time you're about to react in anger, pause. Consider what might be going on in their life. We all see the world differently, and by recognizing this shared human complexity and the limitations of our own understanding, we can cultivate more patience, compassion, and connection with those around us.

Relationships

When you're just getting to know someone, it can be tricky to tell if their behavior is a one-off or a real red flag. Say your date snaps at the waiter—are they just hangry, or is this person actually rude?

To figure it out, try asking about what's behind their actions. Maybe they're having a rough day. Consider patterns rather than single incidents. If you notice a behavior consistently, it's more telling than an isolated occurrence. Pay attention to how they talk about past relationships and whether they take responsibility for their part. Don't ignore your gut, but remember that by considering the bigger picture, you'll get a clearer sense of who they really are, beyond just first impressions or isolated incidents.

+ **Question**

Do I have a healthy
relationship with myself
and others?

⊙ **Keywords**

first impressions,
good impressions,
judgment,
perception,
attributions,
stereotypes

Halo Effect

We assume people we like or think are attractive are also good people.

The **halo effect** is the tendency for our overall impression of someone—if we like them or think they are attractive—to influence how we evaluate their actions. For example, if we have a generally positive impression of someone, we are more likely to attribute positive qualities or outcomes to them, even in unrelated areas. Conversely, if we have a negative impression of them, we may overlook or downplay their positive attributes or successes. This bias can lead us to make broad, oversimplified judgments based on limited information.

Light

Making quick decisions in ambiguous situations, giving others the benefit of the doubt, fostering a sense of trust and credibility

 ## Shadow

Making oversimplified or inaccurate judgments, paying attention to superficial qualities, overlooking nuance, perpetuating stereotypes, misplacing trust

Prompts

1. When meeting new people, do you tend to assume positive traits based on how attractive or charismatic they are?

2. Think about a person you look up to. What qualities or achievements do you find most impressive about them? Have you ever overlooked or minimized any of their flaws or mistakes because of that?

3. Think about a product or brand you love. Do you find yourself ignoring or downplaying negative reviews or information about it?

4. Are there any friends whose negative qualities you ignore because of their positive ones? How might this affect your relationship in the long run?

Life

Say you're shopping for a new laptop and you see a sleek, beautifully designed new model from a well-known brand. The aesthetic appeal and reputation create a positive effect, leading you to feel that the laptop must be high-quality, fast, and reliable. You might be leaning toward buying this laptop over a different model, even if the latter has better specs or reviews. The positive impression created by one aspect of the laptop (design or brand) spills over to your overall perception of the product (performance or reliability).

Other subtle ways the halo effect could be influencing your purchases:

1. Assuming a high-priced item is always better quality, even without researching its features or reviews.
2. Buying a product because an influencer you like endorses it, assuming it must be good based on their recommendation alone.
3. Choosing a restaurant because of its aesthetics or branding, assuming the food will be equally impressive.
4. Buying clothes from a store because the salesperson is attractive or charming, even if the clothes are overpriced or not quite right for you.
5. Choosing a bottle of wine because the label is well designed, even if its reviews are mixed.

Instead of making assumptions and decisions based on limited, peripherally related information, remember to step back, research, and make more objective purchasing decisions.

+ Questions

Where should I live?

Does everything
work out in the end?

⊙ Keywords

retrospection,
predictability,
inevitability,
memory,
justification

Hindsight Bias

**We think things that have already happened were
more likely to happen than things that didn't.**

Hindsight bias is our tendency to perceive past events as having been more predictable than they actually were. We often believe that after an event has occurred, we would have predicted
or even known the outcome before it occurred. This can lead to
overconfidence in our ability to predict future events.

Light

Learning from experience, identifying patterns, justifying past decisions, maintaining self-esteem, enhancing narrative coherence, having improved sense-making, thinking reflectively

 Shadow

Having overconfidence in predictions, oversimplifying causes, misremembering past perspectives, assigning undue blame, underestimating complexity, reinforcing false beliefs

Prompts

1. Have you ever found yourself saying, "I knew it all along," about an outcome that surprised you? What might have contributed to this feeling?

2. When something unexpected happens, either good or bad, do you find yourself looking back and feeling like you had a stronger intuition about it than you really did while it was happening?

3. Have you ever found yourself judging a past decision harshly, even though it made sense based on the information and circumstances at the time? Could you extend compassion to your past self?

4. Reflect on a personal or professional failure. Try to recall the information and emotions you had at the time, and consider whether your current judgment of yourself is fair.

Life

Imagine choosing between two cities: City A, known for its arts scene, diverse culture, and stronger job market, and City B, closer to family, with a lower cost of living and access to nature. You choose City A, but after a year, face unexpected challenges and miss City B's advantages. Looking back, you might think, "I should have known City B was better," overestimating your ability to predict City A's challenges and underestimating potential drawbacks in City B. Instead of dwelling on regret, use this experience to learn about yourself and clarify priorities for future moves. Treat yourself with compassion, acknowledging you made the best choice with the information you had at the time.

Relationships

Imagine you supported a close friend through a tough time, offering help as best you knew how. Looking back, you might feel you could have done more, perhaps having learned about new resources or realizing some comments could have been phrased differently. Try to remember that your past self was doing the best you could with the information and emotional capacity available then. Hindsight bias can make the "right" course of action seem obvious after the fact, but it ignores the uncertainty and complexity at the time. Be gentle with yourself about the past, and use this insight to guide future actions and provide more informed, compassionate support for others and yourself.

Hyperbolic Discounting

We tend to value things that pay off immediately over things that pay off in the future.

Hyperbolic discounting is our tendency to prefer a smaller reward if it's given sooner over a larger reward that's given later, even when the larger reward is objectively better. As the waiting period increases, the reward becomes less and less valuable to us. The term *hyperbolic* refers to the shape of the mathematical curve, which is very steep at first and then gets less steep as the delay gets longer. We have a human preference for immediate gratification. It's easier for us to differentiate between now and next week, and it's harder for us to make a distinction between a year versus a year and a week.

Light

Motivating action, enjoying the present, harnessing unbound creativity, prioritizing passion over patience, utilizing quick decision-making, having flexibility and adaptability, seizing opportunities, encouraging spontaneity

 Shadow

Overspending and undersaving, consuming unhealthily, procrastinating, fostering impulsivity, engaging in reckless pursuits, prioritizing instant gratification, neglecting long-term consequences

Prompts

1. Do your day-to-day choices align with the person you want to become in ten years?

2. When you are tempted to make a choice that brings immediate satisfaction, does your mind also explore and consider the bigger picture?

3. When you're contemplating a big life decision, what gives you more energy: short-term considerations or long-term visions?

4. What types of situations cause you to feel torn between what you want now and what might be better for your future self?

5. How would you describe your relationship with time and making decisions? Does it feel like time influences how you make decisions?

Life

We know sleep is crucial for well-being, productivity, and quality of life, yet we often sabotage our chances of a full night's rest. Your future-oriented brain knows that removing screens from your bedroom, maintaining a consistent evening routine, and moderating caffeine and alcohol intake can improve sleep. However, as night approaches, our short-term brains pull us toward the temptations of scrolling and late-night snacks, preferring easier, tastier, and more entertaining choices. Try to channel your most clear-headed, wakeful future self. Make tactical tweaks like removing your phone charger from your bedroom and putting snacks and drinks in hard-to-reach places. A little friction can go a long way to help you heed your own wise advice: take your time, rest up, and enjoy things with care and moderation.

Relationships

In our teens and twenties, we tend to form close bonds naturally at school and work. As we enter adulthood stages involving careers, marriage, and kids, friendships outside these orbits may fade without the shared gravity of daily interactions. It's easy to postpone nurturing individual relationships, thinking we'll do it later.

A powerful practice is to calculate how many times you might see a given friend over the rest of your lives. You might be surprised to find that it's in the single digits! By enumerating these potential future encounters, you can recalibrate your priorities and invest in your relationships consistently now, rather than relying on an imagined future that may never come.

✳ **Story**

Airport Optimism, pg 101

⊙ **Keywords**

influence,
randomness, luck,
chance, control,
confidence,
predictability

Illusion of Control

We feel like we have more control over events than we do.

The **illusion of control** is our tendency to believe that we have more control over events than we actually do, leading us to overestimate our ability to influence the outcome of a situation or event. In reality, the outcome is largely determined by chance or factors outside our control. This bias is often observed in buying lotto tickets, investing in the stock market, betting on sports, feeling confident in job interviews, taking tests, and waiting for health outcomes—situations where chance plays a big role.

Light

Having increased motivation and confidence, experiencing a sense of agency and empowerment, feeling in control, reducing stress and anxiety in uncertainty, persisting in the face of challenges, taking action and initiative

 ## Shadow

Having blind optimism, underestimating risks and negative outcomes, failing to take precautions, harboring superstitious beliefs, overestimating control over situations, neglecting the role of chance

Prompts

1. How do you feel about the level of control that you have in different areas of your life? Can you notice any recurring themes or patterns in your beliefs?

2. How comfortable are you with uncertainty? In what ways does this comfort or discomfort show up in your decision-making?

3. How do you feel when situations don't go as planned, or when the result is different than you'd hoped?

4. Think about a success and a failure from the last year. How has each shaped your beliefs about how much control you have over situations?

5. Think about a situation where you tried to influence the outcome through magical thinking or superstitious rituals. What emotions or beliefs fueled this behavior, and how did it impact your sense of control?

Life

When negative events happen that are out of our control, it can cause us to ruminate over what-ifs and if onlys. Our wish to control the outcome and avoid something bad or hurtful traps us in regret and self-blame. By keeping the illusion of control in mind, you can maintain a more realistic perspective when in unpredictable situations. When you find yourself thinking "If only . . .," catch yourself and ask, "Even if I did that, would the outcome have changed?" Recognize that the answer is unpredictable, and shift your attention instead to something you can impact.

Money

Investing is an exercise in balancing risk and reward over the long term. Rather than thinking that you can turn a quick profit with your buy-sell timing, remember the inherent uncertainty of investing, and frame it as playing probabilities, not controlling certainties.

Relationships

When deciding if and when it is the right time to become a parent, it's easy to overestimate how much we can control the circumstances or timelines. However, each factor of "being ready" to have kids—whether biologically, economically, or psychologically—is to some extent unpredictable. Rather than getting caught up in trying to get the conditions to their most ideal—the optimal age, career, partner, or moment in life—focus instead on your reasons for wanting a family, your resources and capacity to support your family, and your ability to raise a child. Remember that no perfect path exists, and readiness is always evolving, with trade-offs and randomness at play in every moment.

Illusory Truth Effect

When we see something repeated over and over again, we begin to believe that it's true.

The **illusory truth effect** is our tendency to believe that information is true after we see it many times, regardless of whether it's valid or accurate. This bias highlights the power of repetition and familiarity in shaping our beliefs and judgments. Information that we have heard before seems more plausible and easier to process and understand. Our minds tend to mistake that sense of familiarity as truth, rather than examining the validity and accuracy of the statement. This effect often shows up in news headlines, advertising claims, and misinformation.

Light

Learning through repetition, ensuring consistency in messaging, strengthening belief systems, reinforcing important information, enhancing memory and retention

 ## Shadow

Undermining critical evaluation, distorting views and perceptions, encouraging nondiscernment, accepting fiction as fact, engaging in manipulation and misconceptions, perpetuating misinformation

Prompts

1. How important is firsthand verification to you? Do you accept ideas from trusted sources, or scrutinize all information regardless of its origin?

2. Have your views on key issues shifted from repeated exposure to certain narratives in your social circles? Was this evolution conscious or subconscious?

3. Are there "known truths" you accept without thought? Have you considered examining these beliefs more deeply?

4. Have you ever shared information you've heard repeatedly, despite being unsure of its accuracy? What motivated this?

Life

Social media platforms are filled with trends of all kinds, tailored to your interests. While many are harmless, some can be subtly dangerous, particularly when they offer health and science advice. Juice cleanses, for example, have recently gained popularity, often promoted as a quick fix for weight loss and detoxification. However, these cleanses can pose risks such as causing blood sugar spikes or cleaning out the healthy, good bacteria in your gut as well. Although some people might lose weight during a juice cleanse, this is usually because they're eating far fewer calories, not because juice has special fat-burning properties. It's important to be skeptical of health trends and instead focus on balanced eating and regular exercise for lasting health and well-being.

Money

The rent-versus-buy debate often paints homeownership as the peak of financial wisdom, with renting dismissed as "throwing money away." Take note that the real estate industry profits from this narrative. When mortgage rates soar, the decision becomes more nuanced. It's not just about monthly payments—it's weighing investment opportunities, upfront costs, and the value of ownership against the freedom of renting. Remember, a house isn't just an asset; it's a responsibility. Rather than automatically following conventional wisdom, consider carefully if you're ready to take on all the responsibilities of homeownership.

✳ **Stories**

Trim Grass, pg 73
The Rickshaw, pg 125

⊙ **Keywords**

belonging,
loyalty, identity,
conformity,
norms, groups,
community

In-Group Bias

We favor members of groups we belong to
(the in-groups) over members of groups we don't
(the out-groups).

In-group bias is our tendency to favor our own group over other groups. The categories can be overt, like ethnicity, nationality, and religion, and they can also be subtler, like attending the same school or working at the same company or liking the same sports team. We tend to feel more empathy and loyalty toward those in our in-group and to trust them more. This also means that we can be prejudiced or feel negatively toward the "out-group." Our shared identity shapes our perceptions of others and ourselves.

Light

Creating a sense of belonging, using loyalty to create tighter communities, collaborating with a team to achieve shared goals, experiencing confidence and pride in a group, feeling a sense of purpose and belonging to a group larger than oneself

 ## Shadow

Having a negative attitude and hostility toward those who are different, feeling pressured to conform, creating echo chambers that are sheltered from outside perspectives, lacking trust for those outside the group

Prompts

1. What values, opinions, or beliefs show up in your daily life? Where did these originate?

2. Are you comfortable questioning or deviating from what you see your friends and family doing?

3. Have you felt hesitant to share certain thoughts or parts of yourself to avoid tension or conflict in group conversations?

4. How do you lean into independent thinking and creativity when you make decisions?

5. Who do you give the benefit of the doubt to? How might you be more empathetic with those who feel unfamiliar or different from you?

Work

A company's culture is its personality. It grows from everyone's contributions, but leaders shape it too. Longtime employees often become the face of this culture. However, be careful not to praise only those who fit in perfectly. People who suggest changes can be just as valuable. Remember this when hiring, promoting, or dealing with problems—especially when it involves higher-ups.

Relationships

Family get-togethers can feel like time travel. You're suddenly a kid again, stuck between old arguments and new views. It's easy to defend Mom's point of view or explain away Grandma's behavior with "That's how she was raised" or "She's from a different era." But favoring our own "team" limits everyone's growth. At your next family meal, try to gently investigate more ingrained perspectives. Ask new questions and listen without assuming you know the answers. Look for common ground and shared values, even with relatives who seem different. You might end up understanding others better and learn something new—even from that uncle you usually avoid!

⁜ **Stories**

Buoyancy, pg 51
Mapo Tofu, pg 57

⊙ **Keywords**

isolated choices,
broader context,
collective impact,
goals, patterns

Isolated Choice Effect

We tend to make decisions about our choices in isolation, without considering the larger context or the collective impact of our decisions on our goals.

The **isolated choice effect** is our tendency to choose differently when faced with one decision in the short term, rather than many decisions over the long term. This approach focuses on each choice as an individual event, which can lead to decisions that may not align with our long-term goals. In contrast, by grouping or bracketing our choices across time or instances, we can encourage ourselves to see the forest rather than just the trees.

Light

Focusing on immediate goals, reducing decision fatigue, enabling quick actions, promoting task completion, boosting short-term productivity

 Shadow

Making impulsive decisions, prioritizing immediate goals over long-term goals, overlooking the cumulative impact of choices, using resources inefficiently

Prompts

1. Do you notice any patterns or themes in how you make decisions? Do you tend to think ahead to the future or make decisions moment by moment?

2. Can you identify any recurring decisions in your life that could benefit from being grouped or viewed collectively?

3. Do you find yourself making impulsive choices? How have these decisions impacted your overall happiness and satisfaction?

4. In what areas of your life might you be overlooking the cumulative effect of small, repeated decisions?

5. How could you create a system to regularly review and align your daily decisions with your broader life objectives?

Life

Creating a ritual of meal preparation can lead to healthier food choices, and you'll save money by cooking and eating at home. At the start of the week, find a recipe that you would be excited to have more than once. Choose one that you can easily prepare in a larger batch—look for Instant Pot or one-pan recipes. (I love making ginger chicken rice in a cast-iron pan.) Set aside time in your week to buy or order groceries. When Sunday evening rolls around, prepare your dish for the following week. I like to portion out the leftovers into smaller containers so that I can easily grab and reheat one for lunch.

When we make decisions about what to eat at the beginning of the week, we tend to make healthier choices than when we choose in the moment. This routine can help avoid the last-minute "grab a burger" or other fast option that we often turn to in a pinch. In time, you might find yourself looking forward to the simplicity and ease of your home-cooked meals.

Work

When a company is hiring, it's common for them to search for the very best person for the job, based on the description of the open role. However, if you can consider the existing team's skill set and dynamic, you can make a more holistic decision about who can best complement the larger group. For example, if the team is already strong in technical expertise but could improve their communication skills, hiring a strong communicator could up-level everyone.

✳ **Story**

Good at Quitting, pg 107

⊙ **Keywords**

categorizing,
compartmentalizing,
justification,
framing, value,
deal

Loss Aversion

If we have to choose between avoiding a loss or acquiring an equivalent gain, we'll value avoiding the loss higher.

Loss aversion is our tendency to strongly prefer avoiding losses over acquiring equivalent gains. The psychological pain of losing is about twice as powerful as the pleasure of gaining the same amount. This leads to risk aversion; we often choose to keep everything the same if it means avoiding potential losses, even if taking a risk could lead to significant gains. For example, if someone offered you a bet where you could flip a coin and either win $100 if it lands on heads or lose $100 if it lands on tails, most people would decline the offer altogether because the fear of losing $100 is more intense than the anticipation of gaining $100.

Light

Having prudence, being cautious with risks, valuing stability and security, focusing on gratitude for what you have, fostering commitment and loyalty, avoiding impulsive decisions

 Shadow

Staying in comfort zones, inhibiting growth and progress, having difficulty letting go, being attached to possessions, finding it difficult to change, procrastinating and avoiding, ruminating and hoarding

Prompts

1. Are there areas in your life where you're holding on tightly to avoid loss? What would it look like to loosen your grip on what you're afraid of losing?

2. Imagine the worst-case scenario if you took a risk you're considering. How likely is that to happen? What's the best-case scenario?

3. Think back to a time when you experienced a significant loss. What did you learn about yourself and your resilience when that happened?

4. Is there a possession, relationship, or situation that you're holding on to tightly, even though it may no longer serve you? What makes it difficult to let go?

Relationships

In relationships, we often fear losing approval or companionship. This can make us people-please, avoid conflicts, and put up with bad treatment. We stay quiet about our needs to keep the peace, fearing the loss of the relationship.

To counter this, identify your core needs and dealbreakers. Practice speaking your truth kindly but firmly. It might feel risky at first, as you could lose some approval. But by setting boundaries, you teach others how to treat you. Remember, a short-term loss can lead to long-term gains. Being willing to risk small losses now can create better, more respectful relationships in the future.

Existential

Thinking about death is scary, so we often avoid it. We use distractions like social media to escape this fear and other uncomfortable moments in life. But some spiritual teachings say facing death can actually make life better.

The WeCroak app, inspired by a Bhutanese saying, reminds users five times daily that they'll die. While surprising at first, these reminders can bring peace and perspective. They help us focus on what's truly important instead of getting lost in digital distractions.

Knowing we'll die, what do we want from life? Try writing your own eulogy as if someone who loves you wrote it. What would you want them to say about your life and values? As poet Mary Oliver asked, "What is it you plan to do with your one wild and precious life?"

✳ **Story**

Futureless, pg 145

⊙ **Keywords**

categorizing,
compartmentalizing,
justification,
framing, value,
deal, budgeting,
labeling

Mental Accounting

We tend to think about money differently based on
how we mentally categorize, value, and prioritize it.

Mental accounting refers to the subjective ways we mentally
calculate and categorize money, depending on factors such as
its source, labeling, ease of spending, and whether it was gifted.
This tendency leads to inconsistencies in our cost-benefit
analyses and financial decision-making. For example, we tend
to value money more when it is set aside in a savings or emergency account. Conversely, if we receive an unexpected bonus
or tax refund, we may spend it more frivolously. Similarly, we
might splurge on luxury items while on vacation, even though
we would never pay such high prices at home.

Light

Spending with flexibility, rewarding yourself, allocating money toward goals, splurging intentionally, compartmentalizing financially, effectively budgeting, feeling a sense of security and reduced financial stress

 Shadow

Spending irrationally, having an inconsistent financial outlook, making emotional or frivolous purchases, overspending in certain areas while neglecting others, ignoring fungibility, justifying poor financial choices, hindering financial growth

Prompts

1. Do you notice yourself thinking about money differently depending on how you earned it (e.g., regular income, bonuses, gifts, or inheritances)?

2. How do you categorize your spending? Do you have mental "buckets" for different types of expenses?

3. Would you treat your money differently if it was in one single account rather than in smaller accounts divided by how you earned it and what you intended to use it on?

4. Think of a financial goal such as a down payment or paying off a loan. How might you mentally reframe your income and spending to contribute to this goal more effectively?

Life

Use mental accounting in your favor when it comes to health spending. Consider a company-sponsored FSA (Flexible Spending Account). By allocating money to an FSA, you're essentially creating a separate "mental account" for health expenses. This pre-allocated, tax-free money often makes services like therapy or acupuncture feel more accessible and affordable.

Even though it's still your money, the act of setting it aside in a specific account changes how you perceive and use it. You're more likely to invest in your health because in your mind, that money is already "spent" on healthcare, reducing the perceived cost barrier for these beneficial services.

Relationships

After a long week at work, your partner surprises you with a fancy dinner date, a splurge that feels worth it because you both feel more connected after. The following week, your partner gets a parking ticket and needs some cash to cover it, and you find yourself feeling annoyed at the extra expense.

Pay attention to how you assign value to these different types of spending and how they can create complicated relationship economics. By considering all spending in your relationship equal, you can help smooth out some unevenness in perception and reciprocity.

✳ Story

Airport Optimism, pg 101

⊙ Keywords

continuity,
denial, risk
underestimation,
overoptimism,
complacency,
blind spots,
status quo

Normalcy Bias

We tend to underestimate the likelihood and effect of rare disasters.

The **normalcy bias** is our tendency to assume everything will continue to function as usual, even when the signs of crisis or disaster are imminent. This can lead to a lack of preparation because we are slow to accept that something catastrophic is approaching. Because most of the time things are normal and fine, we tend to rationalize away early warning signs.

Light

Experiencing stability, preventing panic, prioritizing routine, worrying less, feeling comfort, shrugging off minor disturbances, accepting variability, maintaining calm in uncertain times, fostering resilience, being optimistic

 Shadow

Underestimating risk, doing limited preparation, responding with delays, experiencing complacency, having gaps in planning, ignoring warning signs, feeling a false sense of security, resisting change, having difficulty adapting to new realities

Prompts

1. What do you imagine your life will look like in ten years? Twenty years? How much change versus continuity do you envision? What assumptions are you making about stability?

2. When you hear warnings about potential disasters—whether a home fire, an earthquake, or otherwise—do you tend to think that you won't be affected, or do you take action and prepare?

3. How did the COVID-19 pandemic challenge your expectations of normalcy?

4. Make a list of things that you assume will operate smoothly for the next decade, such as transportation, electricity, and the food supply. How could each of these plausibly become more volatile?

Relationships

Transitioning to caring for aging parents with declining health or changing abilities can be challenging for everyone involved. It requires patience from parents adjusting to receiving care, and compassion from adult children learning to be supportive in a new way. When we've viewed our parents as caretakers for most of our lives, it's natural to want continuity in this relationship.

However, resisting necessary changes in living arrangements and daily routines can slow down the transition into these new roles. Instead, find comfort in familiar rituals, favorite meals, and shared memories while embracing this new life stage.

Purpose

It can feel overwhelming to face the many large-scale social, political, and environmental problems that are a part of our reality. It can feel like any one of us isn't capable of enacting a big enough change, and at the same time, that any small actions we take won't matter. Our natural survival response to minimizing risk and continuing as normal nudges us to do what we've always done.

Instead of fixating on problems beyond your control, focus on impactful everyday actions. Volunteer locally, reduce household waste, and support ethical businesses. These small steps create ripple effects benefiting both you and your community. As you develop personal agency, notice what gives you a sense of purpose. Consistent, small actions within your immediate sphere can lead to meaningful change and a greater sense of empowerment.

✳ **Story**

Airport Optimism, pg 101

⊙ **Keywords**

overestimation,
positivity,
confidence,
hope, resilience,
expectations,
underestimating
risk, control

Optimism Bias

We think we're less likely to experience a negative event than other people.

The **optimism bias** is our tendency to overestimate the likelihood that we will experience positive events in the future while underestimating our risk for negative events. It is sometimes referred to as "unrealistic optimism," since we remain positive even when the evidence may not warrant it.

Light

Feeling motivated, setting ambitious goals, being resilient in the face of challenges, having strong coping mechanisms, feeling hopeful, experiencing self-confidence, recovering from setbacks

 ## Shadow

Underpreparing, having unrealistic expectations, engaging in poor risk assessment, overestimating returns, not planning for contingencies, ignoring warning signs, overlooking potential obstacles

Prompts

1. Do you tend to plan for the best-case scenario? Or do you also take steps to prepare for the worst-case scenario?

2. Reflect on a recent decision or situation where you felt particularly optimistic. What contributed to that expectation? How did it turn out?

3. Would your friends and family describe you as an optimist? In what ways does this trait serve you well? Can you think of any situations where it might be creating blind spots?

4. In what areas of your life do you tend to be most optimistic? Are there areas where you're more cautious or pessimistic?

5. How does your optimism affect your relationships? Are there times when it might lead to unrealistic expectations of others?

Life

When reading inspiring books, we often think, "This makes perfect sense! I'll change my life to match these ideas." We optimistically envision ourselves effortlessly implementing these changes. However, this optimism ignores the gap between knowing and doing: real change requires active effort, not just knowledge.

To bridge this gap, take this optimism and use it as motivation to break down lofty goals into small, actionable steps. Consistency and accountability in practicing these steps can gradually turn new behaviors into habits.

Work

For parents, balancing career aspirations with family responsibilities involves significant trade-offs and challenges. Yet when setting career goals, we tend to focus optimistically on best-case scenarios that promise both professional success and perfect work-life harmony.

This overly positive outlook can hinder our ability to realistically plan for the complexities of juggling work and parenting. By recognizing our tendency toward optimism, we can maintain a more balanced perspective and better prepare for the various phases of our career and family life.

+ **Questions**

How do I heal from heartbreak?

How should I spend my holiday, vacation, or time off?

⊙ **Keywords**

peak moments, recall, emotional, retention, memory, intense, vivid, amplification

Peak-End Rule

We tend to remember how experiences felt at their peak and at their end.

The **peak-end rule** is our tendency to judge an experience based largely on how we felt at its most intense point (the peak) and at its end, rather than the average of every moment of the experience. This suggests that the duration of an experience has less impact on how it is remembered, and instead, we tend to rely on the most intense feelings (whether positive or negative) and the final moments of the experience when forming an overall perception of it. This mental shortcut simplifies past experiences, making them easier to recall, rather than considering the average of the entire experience.

Light

Experiencing increased enjoyment and moments of delight, coming to positive conclusions, creating satisfaction, leaving positive impressions, being motivated to finish, focusing on key moments, having positive recall

 ## Shadow

Making skewed judgments of experiences, forgetting prolonged suffering, encouraging preferential treatment, experiencing distorted memory accuracy, neglecting overall quality of experience

Prompts

1. When you reflect on some of your favorite moments or experiences, what sticks out? Does your evaluation stem from the entire experience or certain moments or your mood at the end?

2. How do impromptu or unplanned moments versus meticulously planned experiences impact your memory and feelings of satisfaction?

3. When you reflect on your day, what tends to boost your mood or energy level? How do these things change your overall perception of the day?

Work

Renowned graphic designer Stefan Sagmeister's concept of "radical sabbaticals"—taking one full year off every seven years—exemplifies how structuring time off can create memorable experiences throughout life. This approach distributes retirement, allowing for periodic peaks of renewal instead of one extended period at life's end.

While most can't take year-long breaks, we can apply the peak-end rule to shorter periods. When planning a vacation, schedule a standout "peak" experience midway and a satisfying conclusion. For example, on a week-long trip, plan a thrilling activity like skydiving as your peak, and a reflective sunset picnic as your end. By consciously designing time off with the peak-end rule, even short breaks become extraordinary experiences that fuel motivation long after they're over.

Relationships

When relationships end abruptly, the lack of closure can lead to "ambiguous loss," leaving us searching for answers. Our minds often fixate on the last few painful memories or the big fights and what each person did wrong. However, it's important to intentionally balance these memories with the positive peaks as well.

Closure, or the perceived end of a relationship, is something you can control internally. Try writing a letter to yourself about what you learned and how you grew from the relationship. Reflect on patterns and how the highs and lows shaped your overall feelings.

By recognizing how our memory selectively focuses on certain aspects and acknowledging the challenges of unresolved endings, we can take charge of our healing process and gain wisdom from the experience.

Stories

Hanger Math, pg 67
Slow Shopping, pg 97

 Keywords

justification,
rationalizing,
consistency,
avoidance,
choice-supportive,
retroactive

Post-Purchase Rationalization

When we buy something, we tend to value it more after the fact.

Post-purchase rationalization is our tendency to justify or rationalize our decision to buy after the fact. We might emphasize the positive aspects or overlook any drawbacks of the option we chose. This happens especially with expensive or important purchases to help reduce any anxiety, doubt, or discomfort that we feel and to subconsciously convince ourselves that we made the right call.

Light

Having confidence in purchases, experiencing peace of mind, engaging in justified spending, making the most of purchases, identifying true preferences, investing in quality products, having the courage to make big purchases

 ## Shadow

Ignoring flaws, failing to evaluate objectively, being unwilling to recognize disappointment, overspending beyond budget, clinging to purchases, disregarding negative aspects of the product, having unrealistic expectations

Prompts

1. Think about a product you own but rarely use. What reasons do you give yourself for keeping it?

2. How do you react to buyer's remorse? Do you quickly dismiss your doubts or take the time to think through why you are feeling regret?

3. Think of a big purchase you made that dropped in value or usefulness over time. What did you do when this happened?

4. What is your relationship with purchases that are tied to your identity, like your clothing or style, brands, devices, home decor, or car?

5. How does your mood or emotional state at the time of purchase affect your later satisfaction with the item?

Life

When we splurge on expensive items, especially those that feel thrilling or keep us trendy, we often rationalize the extra cost. Upgrading gadgets or vehicles yearly seems exciting with their new features, but the initial thrill typically fades faster than expected, and the impact on our lives is often less significant than anticipated.

Yet, when asked about our purchase, we tend to justify its usefulness and value. This is post-purchase rationalization bias: our minds, avoiding discomfort, unconsciously defend our buying decisions. While this can temporarily ease our doubts, it hinders honest evaluation of whether our money was well spent.

By allowing ourselves to sit with the discomfort of questioning our choices, we can gain valuable insights. This self-reflection, though challenging, enables us to make more informed decisions in future purchases, potentially saving money and reducing buyer's remorse.

Work

When we make a big career move, there's always a chance that it won't pan out how we'd hoped. We then may struggle to accept that we were wrong to take a big leap of faith. We might give ourselves hopeful justifications to stay, such as "That promotion will come next year" or "Once my manager gets settled in," but consider whether these promises are rooted in reality.

If they aren't, you can accept that you were too optimistic about investing your time and effort in this job. The sooner you realize this, the sooner you can liberate yourself and make a better choice next time. Acceptance of the truth can take effort, but noting your regret is a useful way to make better decisions in the long run.

+ **Questions**

How can I stay more
connected to the
people around me?

How can I be a better
partner, friend, and/or
parent?

⊙ **Keywords**

latest, memory,
recall, weighting,
emphasis

Recency Effect

We tend to remember and care about more recent things.

The **recency effect** is the tendency to place more attention on and give more weight to the most recent information received. We tend to remember and emphasize recent events over ones that happened earlier, which can skew our perception and lead to inaccurate judgments, as we may not consider the full context or the longer-term picture.

Light

Using the latest available information, detecting changing patterns, being responsive to new trends and knowledge, quickly adapting to current conditions

 Shadow

Overweighting short-term trends, neglecting historical context, forgetting important events from the past, overgeneralizing based on recent interactions, underestimating long-term patterns

Prompts

1. Do you find yourself more influenced by the latest news and trends, or do you look at historical context as well?

2. Have you ever made a snap judgment about a person or something based on your most recent interaction?

3. In your relationships, do you ever catch yourself judging the entire connection based on your most recent interaction rather than the full arc of the relationship?

4. Have you ever made a big decision based on a very recent experience, even though it might have been an exception? What emotions were driving your choice?

Life

If you've ever almost gotten into a car accident while driving, you might have noticed that the vivid memory of this near miss subconsciously makes you drive more cautiously for the next few days, as the memory feels very recent. However, as weeks pass without further incident, the impact of that memory starts to fade, and your previous looser driving habits start to resurface.

While it's helpful to drive more carefully in the short term after nearly getting into an accident, it's equally crucial to maintain safe habits even as the intensity of the experience fades. Remember, the risk of an accident is always present on any given day, not just in the aftermath of a close call. By recognizing how recent events can skew your perception of risk, you can consciously work to adopt and maintain safe driving practices for the long term, regardless of the timing of your last near-miss experience.

Relationships

Imagine you haven't seen a childhood friend in years, but you recently had the chance to reconnect over a nostalgic weekend filled with laughter and old stories. In the weeks following this reunion, you might find yourself thinking about this friend more often, focusing on the warmth and joy of your recent interactions rather than the time you spent apart.

This positive focus can inspire you to reach out more frequently, making plans to get together again soon and putting more overall effort into nurturing the friendship. While one great weekend can't erase past distance or disagreements, it can serve as a powerful reminder of why this person is important to you, acting as a catalyst for you to reinvest in the relationship with renewed appreciation and dedication.

※ **Story**

Mapo Tofu, pg 57

⊙ **Keywords**

impulsivity,
self-regulation,
false optimism,
willpower, urges,
overconfidence

Restraint Bias

We think we're better at resisting temptations than we are.

The **restraint bias** is our tendency to overestimate our self-control toward impulsive urges and cravings. We incorrectly assume that we will exhibit more restraint than we have at the moment. This could show up as eating more sweet treats than we planned, spending more money than we budgeted, or choosing fries over salad even though we are trying to eat more healthily. By recognizing that we have less restraint than we think, we can better account for our natural impulsivity.

Light

Motivating preparation, inspiring proactive behavior, fostering resilience against temptation, encouraging ambitious goal-setting

 # Shadow

Experiencing disappointment, making poor choices, feeling regret, assuming control, engaging in impulsive and indulgent behaviors, self-sabotaging, underestimating temptations, having unrealistic expectations, failing to create safeguards

Prompts

1. Think about the last time you successfully made a healthy choice, such as skipping dessert or an alcoholic drink. What helped with restraint?

2. What external controls or accountability partners can you use to help compensate when your willpower needs some extra support?

3. How does your environment (home, work, social settings) influence your ability to exercise restraint? Are there changes you could make to support better self-control?

4. When you give in to temptation, what thoughts, feelings, or emotions do you experience? Can you notice any patterns in these sensations?

Life

We often visit our snack drawer out of habit, not hunger. To improve impulse control, store healthier treats visibly and indulgent ones out of sight. Use opaque containers or portion out snacks to bolster restraint, especially during stressful times or late in the day.

Relationships

When setting up rules for kids, for screen time or any other temptations, you may feel confident that your clear explanations and their cheerful agreement mean they will follow through. By becoming more realistic about our ability to restrain ourselves—especially children, who are even less able to self-moderate—you will feel empowered to set up impartial controls such as an automatic timer to help everyone avoid meltdowns.

Purpose

We tend to overestimate our productivity during free time, dreaming of accomplishing big projects or finding ultimate relaxation. Yet as the weekend or vacation rolls around, distractions tend to steal our focus, which can leave us disappointed with what we actually accomplished. Add gentle structure to your goals, limit commitments, and be compassionate with yourself as you nurture what matters most over time.

✳ **Story**

Hanger Math, pg 67

⊙ **Keywords**

moral licensing,
self-justification,
compensatory
ethics,
indulgence,
rationalization,
moral credentials,
balancing,
good deeds,
transgressions

Self-Licensing Effect

We give ourselves permission to do things we consider "bad" after we've done things we consider "good."

The **self-licensing effect** is our tendency to give ourselves permission to do something bad or immoral after first doing something good. This happens because we feel that we've earned the right to indulge because of our past good deeds, as if the positive behavior "licenses" the negative behavior. This effect can manifest in small ways, like treating ourselves to our favorite indulgence after exercising, or in bigger ways, like engaging in unethical business practices after making a charitable donation.

Light

Enjoying rewards without excessive guilt, finding motivation for positive behaviors, maintaining balance between discipline and pleasure, alleviating the burden of perfectionism, navigating conflicting priorities

 ## Shadow

Justifying questionable choices, acting with entitlement and selfishness, overestimating positive actions, underestimating negative consequences, having a false self-image of virtue

Prompts

1. When have you indulged in an unhealthy habit because you felt you "earned" it through a positive action? How did you justify it to yourself, and how did you feel afterward?

2. Have you ever slacked off on a commitment because you felt your previous efforts earned you a break? Did that align with your goals and values?

3. What patterns do you notice between discipline and indulgence in your life? How might you find a more balanced approach?

4. Are there any behaviors you engage in that don't align with your values but you justify because of your positive actions in other areas?

5. When you've used positive actions to justify nonideal choices, what deeper needs or desires might be driving that behavior?

Life

It's admirable to take steps to reduce your carbon footprint through daily eco-friendly habits. However, it's important to be mindful of self-licensing, where these small actions can justify more significant choices, such as taking long-haul flights.

To counteract this, consider adopting a more holistic view of your environmental impact by examining the carbon footprint of various aspects of your life, including travel, diet, home energy use, and consumption habits. By making consistent, eco-conscious choices across all areas of your life, you can contribute more effectively to a sustainable future. Remember that small green actions, while valuable, don't negate the impact of larger, more carbon-intensive decisions.

Relationships

Imagine a partner who surprises their spouse with a grand gesture, like an extravagant gift or a thoughtfully planned trip. Afterward, they might subconsciously feel entitled to be less attentive or present in the relationship for a while, as if their display of affection has earned them a pass. It's like believing they've overwatered the plant of their relationship, and now it can survive some neglect until the next big effort.

Healthy relationships thrive on consistent nurturing, not a cycle of overcompensation and inattention. Instead of alternating between grand gestures and emotional absence, try to prioritize steady, small acts of love, gratitude, open communication, and quality time together. This daily commitment keeps the relationship thriving without its depending on sporadic, unsustainable efforts to make up for periods of neglect.

★ **Stories**

Airport Optimism, pg 101
Good at Quitting, pg 107
Pentel 0.5mm Lead, pg 151

⊙ **Keywords**

inertia, comfort,
loss aversion,
preference
for stability,
resistance to
change, default

Status Quo Bias

We prefer that things stay the way they are, even if change would be for the better.

The **status quo bias** is our tendency to prefer the way things are currently, and to perceive any change from the baseline as a loss, even when a change might have positive outcomes. We feel inclined toward doing nothing or maintaining a previous decision rather than taking action or making a change. The status quo feels safer and more comfortable than the uncertainty that comes with doing something different.

Light

Experiencing stability and consistency in uncertain times, preserving what's working well, avoiding unnecessary risks, appreciating what you have, maintaining rituals that provide comfort, honoring your past choices

 ## Shadow

Experiencing stagnation, missing opportunities for improvement, fearing change, staying in bad situations, experiencing lack of growth, fearing the unknown, becoming rigid or inflexible, ignoring problems because change feels hard

Prompts

1. What parts of your life feel stagnant or stale right now?

2. Think of a decision you made in the past that you're sticking with out of comfort. What would change if you looked at that choice with fresh eyes?

3. What's a belief, habit, or situation that you'd like to change but haven't? What's holding you back? What's the worst that could happen if you made that change?

4. If your wisest, most objective friend looked at your current life choices and patterns, what would they lovingly suggest you rethink or reinvent?

Work

When starting a new job, you may feel eager to learn the ropes and fit into the existing company culture. You observe how things are done and try to adapt to the established processes and norms. However, as time goes on, you start to wonder if the company's reliance on past processes is more a result of "this is how we've always done it" thinking than intentional strategy.

You realize that your fresh perspective and expertise could potentially help the company run more effectively, even though it might feel uncomfortable to challenge the status quo. Remember, this is likely one of the reasons you were hired—to bring new ideas and perspectives to the table.

Relationships

Family dynamics can become stagnant over time, especially when we fall into the same patterns of relating that we grew up with. We might find ourselves playing out old roles without even noticing it. If you feel like your family interactions have become routine or limiting, consider different ways to shake things up.

You could start by gently suggesting "I know we've always done chores this way, but what if we tried something different this year?" Encourage new traditions or rituals that create space for each person's unique needs and preferences. Small shifts in how we relate can create openings for new dynamics to emerge.

Stories

Hanger Math, pg 67
Good at Quitting, pg 107

 Keywords

investment,
defaults,
opportunity,
unlock, resources

Sunk Cost Fallacy

The more we invest in something, the harder it becomes to abandon it.

The **sunk cost fallacy** is our tendency to make decisions that are influenced by the emotional investments we've made in the past, rather than based on what's best for us in the moment. These investments of time, money, or effort cause us to feel guilty or regretful if we do not follow through. Therefore, the more we invest in something, the harder it becomes to abandon it, even if it's no longer serving us.

Light

Fostering perseverance, encouraging commitment to long-term goals, building resilience, deepening appreciation for effort, cultivating loyalty, inspiring creative problem-solving, motivating follow-through on commitments

 ## Shadow

Being unwilling to make sacrifices in the short term, refusing to adapt to new situations or new ideas, deciding to stay in a situation if unhappy, continuing to spend money on something because an investment has already been made

Prompts

1. Ask yourself "Why should I stay?" rather than "Why should I leave?" Evaluate if the original reasons you were drawn to this commitment are still compelling.

2. Are you bound to any old situations that aren't serving their purpose? What keeps you holding on?

3. What have your past experiences taught you about letting go? How can you apply those lessons to your life now?

4. How can you radically alter your perspective on a current commitment or investment?

5. How do you typically react when faced with the decision to cut your losses? What emotions come up?

6. How might a seemingly negative situation be a blessing in disguise? What is the bright side of this situation?

Life

When you're in a long-term situation like a living arrangement, business, or relationship, take time to reflect. Make a simple list of your initial goals, as if explaining them to a child. Compare your current reality to these goals. Have you compromised on any? Ask yourself: Would I choose this situation again today? Could I excitedly explain why to a friend?

Use this same reflective process before starting new opportunities. Take note of why you're excited, including both existing positive aspects and hoped-for developments. Give yourself a set time frame for learning and living your decision. As you approach this check-in date, compare your initial aspirations with your current reality, using your original reflections as a guide. This practice helps you stay true to your goals and decide whether to stick with something or make changes to better match your values.

Work

The sunk cost fallacy is known for keeping us in jobs longer than we should, but it can also show up in subtler ways, particularly if you've been at the company for a longer time. Close workplace relationships can cloud our judgment. We might overlook a lack of growth opportunities because we're friends with our manager, or even tolerate a difficult coworker due to years of shared history. These emotional investments can trap us in situations that no longer serve us.

Consider how past efforts might be influencing your current choices. Remember, it's okay to reassess and change course, even after years of investment.

✳ **Story**

Trees, pg 85

⊙ **Keywords**

experimentation,
failure, resilience,
overcoming
challenges

Survivorship Bias

When we try to figure out the cause of success, we look at people or solutions that have succeeded but forget to consider those that have failed.

Survivorship bias happens when we focus only on the people or things that "survived" something and overlook those that didn't make it. This bias can skew our judgment in different ways. For example, we might think that a risky move that happened to work out well for someone was brilliant, while forgetting all the times it failed for others. This tendency can cause us to overlook the bigger picture by missing crucial information. By being aware of this tendency, we can take care to look at the "failures," which often have powerful lessons to teach us too!

Light

Learning through challenging
circumstances, encouraging
experimentation and openness
to failure, fostering optimism in
difficult situations, celebrating
success stories

 ## Shadow

Feeling overconfident in risky
approaches, ignoring invisible
failures, having unrealistic
expectations, pursuing quick
fixes, participating in viral
trends and cheat sheets,
drawing false conclusions,
valuing luck over skill

Prompts

1. How did a failure set you up for success later?

2. Who do you look up to as mentors? Have you taken the time to understand the full picture of their experience by becoming familiar with both their failures and achievements?

3. Have you tried asking for advice from a friend who attempted but was unsuccessful at doing something you are interested in pursuing?

4. Can you recognize the role of luck in influencing the outcomes of your decisions?

5. Do you compare yourself with high achievers who "made it"? How could this be impacting your self-perception or motivation?

6. Have you experienced any losses or made mistakes that you might be able to learn from?

Work

Imagine being hired as a new manager of a team, or as a director at a struggling company. You might be eager to revitalize the organization and spend the first few months making observations of teams and employees who are thriving so that you can help others emulate their success. It would make sense to try to optimize other processes based on what has worked for these productive teams!

You also may want to consider learning from those who are struggling or have left the company. This will help you realize which processes and incentives might benefit everyone, not just those who are already doing well. After all, we don't know why those individuals and teams are succeeding—it could be luck or their individual skill; it's an incomplete picture. By looking at both the successes and failures, your conclusions can be more impactful.

Relationships

When people look for relationship advice, they often turn to couples who have been together for a long time, hoping to learn their secrets to success. However, this approach can lead to focusing only on the relationships that "survived" and overlook those that didn't make it. For instance, we might attribute a couple's fifty-year marriage to never arguing, while forgetting the many marriages that ended in divorce despite following the same principle. By ignoring the "failed" relationships, we miss out on crucial information and risk drawing false conclusions. Instead of looking solely to the success stories, consider also getting advice from friends whose relationships didn't work out. Their experiences can help you recognize the role of luck and circumstances in what makes relationships thrive.

Conclusion

W e've made it to the end of our journey together. I hope that you found moments that inspired reflection and a deeper understanding of yourself along the way.

This book, born from a few years of experiments, transitions, and a lifetime of figuring things out, is a collection of my most memorable and transformative experiences (AVAILABILITY BIAS). Each story serves as a lens through which we can examine the nuances of cognitive bias and its impact on our lives (HINDSIGHT BIAS). But I want you to know that this isn't in any way a complete memoir. Like a greatest hits album, it focuses on the moments that taught me the most, while leaving out the less proud, less exciting, and stagnant chapters of my life (SURVIVORSHIP BIAS). There were years when I felt lost, when I acted against my own advice, and when I repeated the same mistakes over and over again. (In these moments, I wish I'd had a Magic 8 Ball that could have given me all the answers.)

As you close this book and reflect on these pages, you may notice yourself seeing these biases in the world around you (ATTENTIONAL BIAS). When this happens, take a moment to pause and let the recognition settle in. Notice yourself noticing. You can be aware of how your brain is working to bring clarity, while simultaneously trusting that you are honing your intuition about how to make choices that align with what you want for yourself. This is the magic of self-discovery: the more you understand about yourself, the more empowered you become to create a life that resonates with you.

I invite you to carry these moments of introspection with you, to share your own experiences, and to write down the stories you'd include in your own book. For there are many more stories to come—stories that I couldn't capture in the time I had, stories lost to memory or where my writing failed me. But I am grateful to have you along in this experiment with me—my first toe-dip into writing and illustrating.

As you continue on your path, remember to pause and reflect on your biases. Ask yourself the questions that will guide you toward where you want to go. And know that with each decision you make, you move closer to the life that you have been searching for.

Acknowledgments

Thank you to the moon to Lindsay Edgecombe for always believing in me. For years of kind and honest support and for helping shape this from start to finish. Writing this book with your guidance has been transformative.

To Nina Shield, for seeing this for what it could be. To my editor Lauren Appleton and the team at TarcherPerigee, thank you for your patience and heart in the final act.

Buster Benson, thank you for being an incredible friend and mentor. Your work was the seed for this project, and your support helped it grow. To the Rickshaw, thank you for being my all-hours group therapy. Ash, for your tender words that opened me up to what was there. Christin, for your steadfast feedback. Miri, Kevin, Carrie.

Grace Sun and Kevin Jones, thank you for being my number-one cheerleaders; our Brooklyn walk 'n' talks put the wind back in my sails. Christine Cha, for being my first creative partner; our adventures gave me life. Your playful illustrations were what got this all started. Karen Hong, thank you for the incredible bias icons. You both now know more about biases than you ever wanted, ha!

To all the designers: Ryan Putnam, Justin Graham, Meher

Goel, Rodrigo Corral, Drew Heffron, Jack Fulton, Jo Luo, Ryan Mather, May-Li Khoe, Elizabeth Goodspeed, Alicia Tatone. Danny Jones, Tamara Chu, and the TMI crew, for my first reading.

I'm grateful to Ash Huang and Casson Rosenblatt for talking to me about motherhood. Carmen Lau, my first beta reader, your detailed notes were a salve for my anxiety. Kat Li, Elizabeth Weingarten, Mike Byrne, Zach Adams, Philip De Guzman, for your thoughts on early versions.

Hsu Ken, thank you for teaching me how to quit. Didn't think I'd write a book about it, eh? :) To my managers, Shannon Shaper and Frank Yoo, thank you for shaping my path.

Thank you to Rosie, Harrison, and Townes for farmhouse visits and to Mika Sasaki, for my Tokyo writing retreat. Special love for Charlie's crew, who took the best care of him: June and Darren, Meredith and Lily, Victor and Connie, Carmen and Nick.

Gratitude to my generous patrons for giving me an audience and for supporting my years of exploration: Kim Hutchinson, Alexander Romero, Peter Wang, Chaitanya Mendu, Kevin Garcia, Tali Rapaport, Roger Leng, Surya Anand, Jenni Wu, Shefali Netke, Blaise Santiago, Tim Drabandt, Abigail Readey, Ryan Consbruck, Joey Banks, Kaisen Lin, Tina Liu, Leslie Chicoine, Gary Jense, Mind Apivessa, Travis Brimhall, Tim Kim, Robin MacPherson, Connor Bär, Greyson MacAlpine, Max Wendkos, Ann Tai, Matthew Paul, Poz Long, Nata Suu, Alexander Dreymann, Dot Dotter, Andrew Broman, Julia Grebenstein, Michael Wang.

This work was inspired by Daniel Kahneman, Amos Tversky, Esther Perel, Katy Milkman, Ken Liu, Maya Shankar, Andy Puddicombe, Krista Tippett, Pádraig Ó Tuama, Sheila Heti, Ezra Klein, Yancey Strickler, Alexis Madrigal.

To my family: Mom, Ben, Aimee, Jack, Micah, Cap, and Charlie. You are the story behind every story.

Glossary of Biases

Thank you to Buster Benson for allowing me to reference his Pocket Biases definitions. If you'd like to learn more about cognitive biases, you can visit: https://buster.wiki/biases/

A

 Affective forecasting, pg 158: When we try to predict how we'll feel about something in the future, we tend to overestimate both the intensity and duration of our emotional reactions.

 Ambiguity effect, pg 161: We choose options that are more certain, even if those options are likely to be worse.

 Anchoring effect, pg 164: We rely too heavily on the first piece of information we receive when making decisions.

Anthropomorphism: We apply human qualities to nonhuman entities.

Apophenia: Our tendency to interpret a vague stimulus as something known to us, such as seeing shapes in clouds, seeing faces in inanimate objects or abstract patterns, and so on.

 Appeal to novelty, pg 167: We think new things are more valuable than the same thing that's older, even if that's the only difference between them.

 Appeal to probability, pg 170: The mistaken assumption that if something is likely to happen, it's definitely going to happen. Murphy's Law is an example of this.

Armchair fallacy: We're more confidently critical about other people's work than we would be if we were actually doing the work ourselves, even when we are less informed about the subject area than the people whose work we are criticizing.

 Attentional bias, pg 173: If we think about something, we'll notice it more in our day-to-day.

Attribute substitution: When we have to make a daunting decision about something, we'll often substitute a simpler problem that we can resolve more easily.

Authority bias: We think the opinions of people who have authority over us are more likely to be correct. A variant, HiPPO, stands for "the highest paid person's opinion."

 Availability bias, pg 176: We tend to favor options that come to mind easily. Things that don't, for whatever reason, are at a severe disadvantage.

B

Backfire effect: When confronted with information that challenges our beliefs, we sometimes reject the information and decide to hold on to our existing beliefs even more strongly. Also called the boomerang effect.

Bandwagon effect: The rate of uptake of beliefs, ideas, fads, and trends increases the more that they have already been adopted by others.

Barnum effect: When we hear something vague that's supposedly about us, we give it high ratings on accuracy. This effect can provide a partial explanation for the widespread acceptance of some paranormal beliefs and practices like astrology, fortune-telling, aura reading, and some types of personality tests. Also known as the Forer effect.

Base rate fallacy: We usually don't consider how likely something is to randomly occur. For example, if having a certain illness is rare, false positives might be more likely than true positives.

Belief perseverance: We tend to avoid revising our past or current beliefs, even when presented with new evidence that contradicts them. Meaning, even after we've officially decided to change our mind about something, some parts of the old belief will linger.

 Bizarreness effect, pg 179: We tend to remember unusual, strange, or peculiar things instead of more mundane, everyday information.

Bucket error: We will choose to reject certain ideas because we wrongly think they conflict with our other beliefs, when they actually don't. For example, when someone believes that being a good writer and being good at spelling must go together, they've created a bucket error by forcing these separate skills into the same mental "bucket."

C

Cathedral effect, pg 182: Working in spaces with high ceilings has a positive effect on creativity, and vice versa.

Change blindness, pg 185: We can only pay attention to a couple of things at once, so we become blind to things that would otherwise grab our attention.

Chesterton's fence: We sometimes avoid addressing problems because we assume they are there for good reasons.

Choice-supportive bias: When we do something, we like to stay loyal to those choices and come up with reasons why they were the right choice after the fact. Choice-supportive bias is the general tendency here, and **post-purchase rationalization, pg 251** is a more specific version that applies to things we buy.

Clustering illusion, pg 188: We tend to see clusters and streaks in data that aren't really there.

Confabulation: We spontaneously create fabricated, distorted, or misinterpreted memories about ourselves and the world without intending to, mostly to fill in gaps in justification and reasoning. Sometimes known as false memory.

Confirmation bias, pg 191: We interpret information in a way that confirms our existing beliefs.

Conservatism: We don't seem to revise our past beliefs quite enough when presented with new evidence that contradicts them. Meaning, even after we've officially decided to change our mind about something, some parts of the old belief will still linger.

Contrast effect: When two things are juxtaposed or sequential, we perceive an exaggeration of the differences between them.

Cryptomnesia: We sometimes think we've come up with something new and original when really it was a forgotten memory that returned without our recognizing it.

Curse of knowledge: When you assume that everyone you're talking to has the same understanding of things that you do.

D

Denomination effect, pg 194: We're less likely to spend large denominations than small ones, even if the amount is the same.

Disposition effect: The tendency to hold on to investments that are doing well and sell those that aren't.

Dunning-Kruger effect, pg 197: When those of us who lack skill or knowledge tend to overestimate our abilities, and those of us with more knowledge or skill tend to underestimate them.

Duration neglect: When enduring a difficult situation, the length of the tough situation matters less to us than the peak and the end. A more general form of the **peak-end rule, pg 248.**

E

 Effort justification, pg 200: When we work for something, we end up valuing it more. Some people also refer to this as the IKEA effect.

Egocentric bias: We sometimes rely too heavily on our own perspective and have a higher opinion of ourselves than we'd have about someone else who was exactly like us.

Empathy gap: When we're angry, it's tough for us to empathize with thinking that we'd have when calm, and vice versa.

 Endowment effect, pg 203: We value things that we own more than what we don't, regardless of the real value of the items.

F

Fading affect bias: We tend to forget memories associated with negative emotions more quickly than memories associated with positive emotions. The result is that we think of the past more fondly than we did at the time we were experiencing it.

 Focusing illusion, pg 206: We tend to place too much focus on one aspect of a decision, while neglecting other crucial factors. This narrow focus can distort our thinking and lead to inaccurate conclusions.

Framing effect: We'll make different choices about information depending on whether it is presented to us in the context of a loss or a gain.

Frequency illusion: When we first learn about something, we start to see that thing everywhere. For example, if you just learned about this illusion, it's possible that you'll start to see examples of the frequency illusion in lots of other places. A more specific form of **attentional bias, pg 173.**

 Functional fixedness, pg 209: We tend to use an object only for its intended purpose.

 Fundamental attribution error, pg 212: We tend to attribute other people's behavior to their personality rather than to external circumstances.

G

Gambler's fallacy: We tend to think that if something is happening more frequently than normal during a given period, it will happen less frequently in the future (or vice versa).

Group attribution error: We tend to think people in a group will have characteristics and behaviors typical to the group.

H

Halo effect, pg 215: We assume people we like or think are attractive are also good people.

Hard-easy effect: We overestimate our ability to achieve hard tasks and underestimate our ability to do easy tasks.

Hindsight bias, pg 218: We think things that have already happened were more likely to happen than things that didn't.

Hot-hand fallacy: If we're experiencing a lucky streak, we believe we have a greater probability of success in further attempts.

Hyperbolic discounting, pg 221: We tend to value things that pay off immediately over things that pay off in the future.

I

IKEA effect: We place a much higher value on things that we built ourselves. Also known as **effort justification, pg 200**.

Illusion of control, pg 224: We feel like we have more control over events than we do.

Illusory correlation: We think two things are connected and meaningful more often than they are.

Illusory superiority: We overestimate our qualities and abilities relative to how we estimate other people with the same qualities and abilities. Also known as the **Dunning-Kruger effect, pg 197**.

Illusory truth effect, pg 227: When we see something repeated over and over again, we begin to believe that it's true.

Immune neglect: When we think of our future emotional state, we don't take into account the impact of our defense and coping mechanisms. A more general version of **affective forecasting, pg 158**.

Impact bias: We overestimate the length and intensity of events that we haven't experienced yet. A part of **affective forecasting, pg 158**.

Implicit stereotypes: We unconsciously attribute to individuals of a group qualities and characteristics that we believe the group to have. Also known as implicit bias.

Information bias: We continue to seek out clarification and information even if it won't impact decisions or actions.

In-group bias, pg 230: We favor members of groups we belong to (the in-groups) over members of groups we don't (the out-groups).

Isolated choice effect, pg 233: We tend to make decisions about our choices in isolation, without considering the larger context or the collective impact of our decisions on our goals.

L

Lake Wobegon effect: On average, we all tend to think we're above average.

Law of the instrument: If we have a tool, we'll fit the problem to be solvable by that tool. If you have a hammer, everything is a nail.

 Loss aversion, pg 236: If we have to choose between avoiding a loss or acquiring an equivalent gain, we'll value avoiding the loss higher.

M

Magical number 7±2: The number of objects the average mind can hold at once in working memory is seven, plus or minus two.

Memory inhibition: We tend not to remember details that we perceive as irrelevant. Sometimes called the Google effect when related to looking things up online.

 Mental accounting, pg 239: We tend to think about money differently based on how we mentally categorize, value, and prioritize it.

Mere exposure effect: We tend to develop a preference for things merely because we are familiar with them. This is one way things like advertising can influence us, by repeating a message that we don't agree with but become familiar with.

Money illusion: People become anchored to prices rather than their purchasing power. This is why it's tough to raise prices even if inflation is moving up faster than prices.

Murphy's law: We tend to attribute bad luck to a perversity of the universe that ensures that anything that can go wrong will go wrong. A subset of the **appeal to probability, pg 170**.

N

Naive cynicism: We think others are more selfishly motivated than we are.

Naive realism: We think we see the world around us objectively and that people who disagree with us must be uninformed, irrational, or biased.

Negativity bias: Even when two or more things are of equal intensity, the ones with a more negative nature (e.g., unpleasant thoughts, emotions, or social interactions; harmful/traumatic events) have a greater effect on our psychological state and processes than the neutral or positive things.

Neglect of probability: We don't understand the probability of risks very well when it's anything other than super high or super low.

Normalcy bias, pg 242: We tend to underestimate the likelihood and effect of rare disasters.

O

Occam's razor: We like to believe that simpler solutions are more likely to be correct than complex ones. Also known as the law of parsimony.

 Optimism bias, pg 245: We think we're less likely to experience a negative event than other people.

Ostrich effect: The tendency to avoid information that we don't want to hear.

Outcome bias: We have trouble evaluating the quality of a decision after we know the results of it, even though the results weren't known at the time the decision was made. Also known as the resulting fallacy.

Out-group homogeneity bias: We see people outside our group as being more similar to one another than people in our groups ("They're all alike; we're diverse").

Overconfidence effect: Our confidence in the accuracy of our judgments is consistently greater than the objective accuracy of those judgments.

P

 Peak-end rule, pg 248: We tend to remember how experiences felt at their peak and at their end.

Pessimism bias: We exaggerate the probability that negative things will happen to us.

Picture superiority effect: We are generally better at remembering images than words.

Placebo effect: If we think a treatment is going to help us, we tend to report feeling better even if it had no direct effect.

Planning fallacy: We tend to underestimate how long something will take. A version of **optimism bias, pg 245**.

Positivity effect: When we like someone, we attribute their good behaviors to their inherent qualities and their bad behaviors to external circumstances, and vice versa for people we don't like.

Post-purchase rationalization, pg 251: When we buy something, we tend to value it more after the fact. A more specific version of choice-supportive bias.

R

Reactance: A negative reaction we feel when we perceive that someone is taking away our choices or limiting the range of alternatives. Leads some to use reverse psychology to take advantage of this effect.

Recency effect, pg 254: We tend to remember and care about more recent things.

Restraint bias, pg 257: We think we're better at resisting temptations than we are.

Rhyme as reason effect: We tend to believe that rhyming statements are more meaningful or accurate or truthful than those that don't rhyme.

Risk compensation: A theory that suggests we adjust our behavior based on the perceived level of risk. We are more careful when we sense greater risk and less careful when we feel more protected. This leads to an overall reduction in the effectiveness of added safety measures, since we compensate by becoming a bit more reckless.

S

 Self-licensing effect, pg 260: We give ourselves permission to do things we consider "bad" after we've done things we consider "good." Also called the moral credential effect.

Spacing effect: We learn better when studying is spaced out over time.

Spotlight effect: We think people are paying more attention to us than they really are.

 Status quo bias, pg 263: We prefer that things stay the way they are, even if change would be for the better.

 Sunk cost fallacy, pg 266: The more we invest in something, the harder it becomes to abandon it.

 Survivorship bias, pg 269: When we try to figure out the cause of success, we look at people or solutions that have succeeded but forget to consider those that have failed.

Swimmer's body illusion: When we confuse selection factors for results. For example, we think if we start swimming, we'll become like a professional swimmer. But in fact professional swimmers tend to be people who already had many of the traits needed to become professional swimmers.

T

Telescoping effect: We perceive recent events as more remote than they are and distant events as more recent than they are.

Time discounting: We value things in the present more than things in the future. A kind of **affective forecasting, pg 158**.

Time-saving bias: We overestimate how much time will be saved or lost by changing our speed.

Tip of the tongue phenomenon: That weird feeling of failing to retrieve a word from memory, combined with partial recall and the feeling that you're going to remember it very soon.

U

Unit bias: Our strong preference to complete whatever we're doing before stopping or starting something else.

V

Von Restorff effect: Hedwig Von Restorff put a name to the phenomenon of how, in a list of things that have something in common, if one item is different, it will be more likely to be noticed. For example, in the list "desk, chair, bed, table, chipmunk, dresser, stool, couch," you are likely to notice and remember the chipmunk more than the others. Also known as the isolation effect.

W

Well-traveled road effect: We estimate that travel time on frequently traveled routes will be less than our estimates of traveling on unfamiliar routes, even if they're the same distance.

Z

Zero-risk bias: We tend to prefer the complete elimination of a risk even when alternative options produce a greater reduction in risk. For example, when people were asked if they prefer the option to decrease a given risk from 5 percent to 0 percent or to decrease a risk from 50 percent to 25 percent, they preferred the idea of 0 percent, despite the drop from 50 percent to 25 percent being a far greater reduction in risk.

Zero-sum bias: Our tendency to judge non-zero-sum situations (where a win-win is possible) as zero-sum (where someone must win and someone must lose).